DARK SIDE
OF THE MITTEN

CRIMES OF POWER
& POWERFUL CRIMINALS
IN MICHIGAN'S PAST & PRESENT

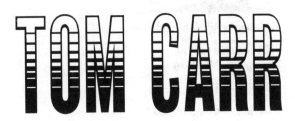

MISSION POINT PRESS

Readers are encouraged to go to
www.MissionPointPress.com to find
information on how to buy this book
in bulk at a discounted rate.

MISSION POINT PRESS

Published by Mission Point Press
2554 Chandler Lake Rd.
Traverse City, MI 49686
(231) 421-9513
www.MissionPointPress.com
Series editor: Heather Lee Shaw
Book design by Heather Lee Shaw
ISBN: 978-1-950659-76-0
Library of Congress Control Number:
2020946794

Printed in the United States of America.

CONTENTS

SENSATIONS OPEN TRIAL OF PURPLES

Attorney For Jacoby Accuses Martel of 'Double-Cross.'

CHENOT CHARGES 'TRIBUTE' GRAFT

Bombings Blamed on Labor Leader by Gang Counsel.

page 42
(Detroit Free Press, June 5, 1928)

INTRODUCTION

AS I WRITE THIS INTRODUCTION, MICHIGAN GOVERNOR GRETCHEN WHITMER WAS RECENTLY THE TARGET OF A KIDNAPPING PLOT BY DOMESTIC TERRORISTS. If I were just starting to write this book, I would include that as a chapter here. However, I started writing *Dark Side of the Mitten: Crimes of Power and Powerful Criminals in Michigan's Past and Present* in late summer of 2019 and wrapped it up in late 2020.

That story would fit this book, as it involves a person or people in power. Not all of the people in power in this book are perps. Some are victims, like the Bay City tycoon who was shot while taking a walk back in the early 20th Century. In addition, not all the things highlighted in this book are actual crimes. Dr. John Harvey Kellogg espoused some strange and even harmful beliefs, though none of them were actual crimes. Still, his and his brothers' fame make their quirks and toxic relationship relevant to this book.

At the time I committed to writing the book for Mission Point Press, I knew it would be topical to look back at the lesser known aspects of some of the best-known names in Michigan. That's because the stories in this book are about the unsavory, the quirky, or the downright ghastly actions of some of this state's immortal figures.

It's more by coincidence than design that *Dark Side of the Mitten* hits bookstores as statues are being knocked down and institutions renamed as a reckoning of this country's deepest self-inflicted wounds. It comes as the Washington Redskins have dropped the racial-slur from their name and are temporarily the Washington Football Team.

And so, is this compilation an attempt to bring down some of Michigan's heroes through the ages? My intention is not to advocate for or against toppling statues or renaming buildings or roads. Personally, I prefer to keep the statues and knock down pedestals.

It's really more of a reminder that there's a yin and yang to everybody. As power grows, so does one's ability to wreak havoc.

That even goes for people related to me. In fact, researching this book particularly hit home as I also discovered information that tainted someone who is something of a family hero.

When I was a kid, my father told me, proudly, that his father's cousin had achieved the impressive position of Chief Justice of the Michigan Supreme Court. I never met Leland Carr, but it was a tidbit that would come up every so often, and I might tell someone of my successful relative.

(Check out my genes, right?) Yet now I find that earlier in his career, in the late 1920s, he ordered Rev. Earl Little, a Black man, and his family to move out of a house in Lansing that they owned, because it was in a White neighborhood. His decision was rendered moot, as racist vandals burned the house down before the family had a chance to move. I admit I haven't studied the aggregate of his career, but this ruling seems unfathomably wrong-headed in our day and age.

I conceived this book after hearing of two of the people I have included in these chapters. They are Albert Molitor, the baron of Rogers City, and Harry Bennett, Henry Ford's right-hand man, union buster and pugilist. The idea was to give an alternative to what most of us know about Michigan's most influential people throughout its known history. Yet in this bizarre phenomenon that is A.D. 2020, much of what is in these pages has become more relevant than ever, and not just because of the plot to kidnap Gov. Whitmer. This year also saw Whitmer change the name of the Lewis Cass office building in Lansing because Cass, a governor of Michigan Territory a U.S. senator, and a U.S. Secretary of State, was also a slave-owner.

Still, only one chapter was actually a result of the headlines. As we quarantined and agonized over Covid-19, I became interested in how the cholera and flu epidemics of the 19th and 20th centuries affected the people of the state, so I added a chapter on that.

I kept the connecting threads somewhat loose, but I hope that the stories inform and entertain in a way that sheds light on pieces of this state's past, as they did for me while I researched them.

While I don't hold back on including opinions in these stories, I have pieced together sources in order to present the past in a factual way. I hope that it helps bring to life certain people, times and places, with some perspective from our own 21st Century perch. In other words, I have peeked behind some of the curtains and hope to reveal to you what I've found.

Thank you for picking up this book and I hope you enjoy it and find it informative.

Tom Carr, October, 2020

OWING THEIR SOULS TO THE COMPANY STORE

WHERE: ROGERS CITY
THE CRIME: MURDER

ALBERT MOLITOR CAME TO THE ROCKY, NORTHWESTERN SHORES OF LAKE HURON TO HARVEST THE WHITE PINES, BUILD A SETTLEMENT IN A FAR-FLUNG AREA OF THE WORLD, AND TO RULE THE TOWN LIKE A RUTHLESS, UNCHECKED BARON.

Molitor came to the area from Wurttemberg, Germany, cutting an impressive figure, with wavy hair, bushy sideburns, a moustache and a vertical soul patch, definitely before they called it a soul patch, or a jazz dot, and most likely before they called it a flavor saver. (It was likely referred to as a mouche in those days.) People said that royal European blood coursed through his entitled veins. They didn't necessarily intend that myth as flattery. His enemies (and he had many) said he was the illegitimate son of King Wilhelm I von Wurttemberg of Prussia, conceived in a romp with a (gasp!) lowly maid.

Molitor had served in the army in Germany, though rumors had him fleeing to America to escape charges of treason at home. He crossed the Atlantic as our Civil War began and enlisted as a first lieutenant in the Union Army, a New York battery. Once again, scandal chased him out: In 1862, the Army accused him of stealing a horse, then dropped the charges and discharged him honorably. Turns out the officer who accused the lieutenant of the crime did it because he just plain didn't like him. That puts the officer in the exclusive company of pretty much anyone who'd ever met Albert Molitor.

By the end of the decade, Molitor had found his way to Detroit, and onto a surveying team that sailed up the Huron shore to explore what riches might hide in the rocks, hills and trees, and to figure out what the investors could build or dredge to make it easier for ships to come and get the merchandise.

Land went cheap in those days. Also, the government offered favorable terms on homesteaded acreage to veterans of the Civil War and the War of 1812. In the last two years of the 1860s, Molitor bought up more than 2,200 acres, much of it from veterans.

Lumber barons and baron-wannabes were throwing money at Michigan's vast forests and getting a lot more back. Molitor partnered with William Rogers, who helped bankroll the lumber camp/sawmill enterprise they called Rogers-Molitor Company. While Rogers stayed in Detroit finding customers for their timber, Molitor ruled the roost up north in what became known as

1

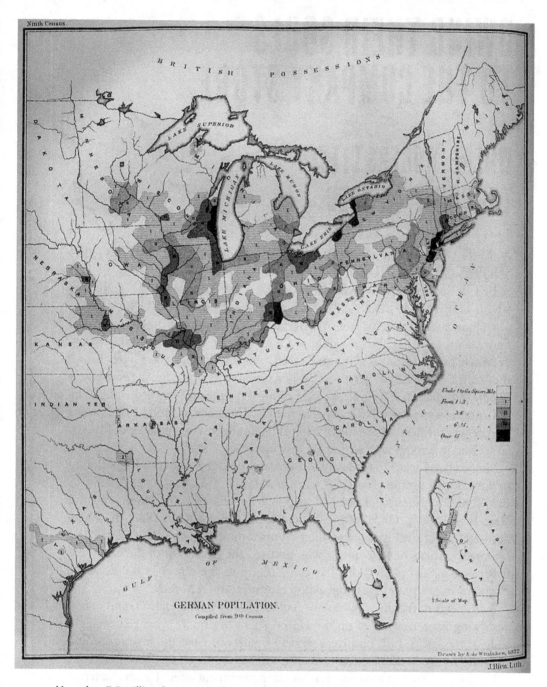

GERMAN POPULATION.
Compiled from 9th Census.

More than 7.5 million German people moved to the United States in the half-century between 1820-1870. Many came to Michigan, including to Rogers City and many other places up the Lake Huron shoreline.

Rogers City. Even though he inspired the town's name, Rogers barely spent any more time in that bucolic backwater than George Washington ever did in Washington State.

In the early 1870s, German immigrants flocked in from Europe, providing labor for Molitor's small local empire. The new immigrants sawed logs for Molitor, planted farms and built log houses. The constant flow of logs out of Rogers City put dollars in the pockets of the investors, and that kept everyone happy. Well, everyone who had a voice anyway.

Molitor was free to rule as he pleased, and he played a hands-on role. A lot of women thought it was too hands-on. He reigned as a tyrant and preyed on employees' sisters, daughters and wives.

He also stacked local government positions with his cronies and monopolized the retail market. The Rogers-Molitor company store offered one-stop shopping—as in there's only one place to shop for flour or lard or other essentials. Good thing people could also hunt, trap and occasionally trade with the Ojibwa and Odawa people of the area. As far as money goes, well, the workers had none unless they were getting it somewhere other than the Rogers-Molitor Company. The boss paid his workers in bogus legal tender known as "scrip," which they could spend at the company store though it had no more value than a "free hug" coupon anywhere else in the world.

When another German immigrant, Herman Hoeft, opened a competing general store, Molitor crushed him with ease. Rogers citizens had plenty of scrip in their pouches, but little cash that would do Hoeft any good. Hoeft figured he could charge his customers in scrip and then trade that to Rogers-Molitor for cash. Little surprise, though, that when

The only known photograph of Albert Molitor, when he was in the German military. He's probably about 19 here and may or may not be thinking about becoming a tyrant. (Presque Isle County Historical Museum)

Hoeft tried to redeem the worthless scrip, Molitor told him to get lost. Even Molitor had no use for his own play money. Hoeft sued, but Molitor owned the judges.

Meanwhile, Molitor had his hand in the local tax grab bag up to his elbows. The county was taxing its citizens for a supposed $30,000 project to build a system of roads. That would be like half a million bucks today, and Albert made sure that pretty much all that tax money landed right in his own pocket.

In Molitor's world, women were nothing more than another resource for him to lord over, just like tax dollars, trees and human toil. One instance people still talk about is when he saw a photograph of Hortensia Carle in the possession of her brother, a Rogers-Molitor employee. The image on the sepia-toned tintype stirred a powerful yearning, as he paid to have Hortensia board a ship for the New World. When she got here, he hired her as his servant. Soon, she became pregnant, and Molitor promised to marry her.

Always the romantic and the gentleman, Molitor took his betrothed on a 250-mile sleigh ride, through snowy woods, farms and villages, all the way to Detroit. Once they got to the big, gaslit city, he pulled the sleigh up to a street corner, kicked her out into the snow and took off, back north to his barony.

At one point, police arrested him, briefly, on the charge of 'being the paternal ancestor of an infantile incumbrance.' Meanwhile, Hortensia,

the mother of said infantile incumbrance, sued him and won a judgment that he owed her $10,000. Hopefully, she was happy enough with her moral victory, because this was Albert Molitor. He never paid her a dime.

Molitor probably thought he would remain untouchable, but the anger and outrage of the town began to rise above a simmer. It rumbled straight out of the morning stillness one August day in 1875, as the Molitor household awoke to the flickering light of torches and shouts about money, roads, and "Let's get the crook!" Molitor rose and grabbed a shirt, then peered out the window to see dozens of people—must've been about two-thirds of the town—some armed,

shouting for him to come out and face them.

He opened the door and stepped out, staring down the apparent leaders. Stone-faced, he listened, as they demanded to see county financial records.

"Where are the roads?" one man asked. They were still no more than trails.

"Where's all the money we paid in taxes?" asked another.

Calm and without expression, he listened to their arguments and grievances. As he gave them no answers, they gradually ran out of steam. They'd done all the talking, so now, they craned their ears awaiting his response.

"Go to Hell," he said.

Their faces turned red. Some surged ahead, wanting to tear him limb from limb, as others held them back. A group of men pulled Molitor out into the street, as one man held up a noose.

"Show us the numbers! Give us some proof! Turn over those books or we'll hang you," they demanded.

Molitor laughed and opened his shirt collar. "Go ahead with your hanging," he spat.

He had called their bluff. He was supposed to cower and give up the evidence, or plead for their forgiveness. Now, their hesitation gave him a foothold and a day-long stalemate began.

The battle of wills outlasted the dew of the morning, then the high, hot sun, and the lengthening shadows of afternoon. As the men of the town leaned on their weapons, wiped their brows and listened to their rumbling stomachs, Molitor ordered a table for one be set in the middle of the street. Unflapped, he sat down and enjoyed a hot dinner, letting the smell of meat and potatoes hit the senses of the hot, tired citizens who were hungrier now for dinner than they were for justice. After he wiped his chin and burped, Molitor watched them slink away in defeat, a smile twitching at the corners of his mouth.

He had won this battle, and he grew bolder. At the same time, those around him grew angrier, and not just his employees. His first wife divorced him for behaving like a tomcat in rut. William Rogers finally dissolved the business partnership as complaints reached his ear. The partners and suppliers he cheated stopped doing business with him. Workers found out he was charging them more for the paltry store items than he was clocking in wages for them. When they lined up to get their seasonal pay, some were told they owed money to their bosses.

Citizens still saw no improvements to the roads, nor one dollar of their 30 grand. Lawsuits piled up like boards from the sawmill and women he harassed had had enough.

Such resentment and ill-wishes hid under just about every hat in town that an angry group—smaller than the previous one, but much more determined—came to his window after dusk on an August night. This time, they had firearms and weren't there to waste time shouting and pleading.

A young clerk named Frederic Larke in Molitor's office may have known about their impending arrival, as he suddenly realized he'd left his coat several doors down the block. Molitor and bookkeeper Edward Sullivan barely noticed as they worked away by kerosene lamp.

The window crashed in toward them as the armed mob announced their presence with blasts of lead. Molitor fell over a chair and onto the floor. Before he realized the danger, Sullivan turned toward the window just as a shot blew him backwards.

"Kate!" Molitor yelled for his sister-in-law, who was upstairs. As she heard the shots, Kate hit the floor. She tried to catch her breath as she faintly heard Albert yell again.

"Kate!" She heard the pained and frantic cry from below.

"Kate!" he managed to gasp out. "I'm dying!"

Mr. Larke, the young man whose life may have been spared by his coat emergency, heard the shots and the glass shattering from down the street. He ran for the sheriff's house. He frantically told him of the "row" at the store. He gasped out what was happening, then ran to get Dr. Simon from his office at the International Hotel.

While word was spreading through town, Molitor lay half under his desk, moaning in pain with his back now full of lead from a shotgun. Sullivan touched the bloody side of his face, where a slug had smashed into his jaw and ripped his tongue off. He struggled toward the stairs and mustered all of his strength to pull himself up to the second floor, spilling a trail of blood. Sullivan died a couple of days later.

Molitor hung on. His brother Edward received word in Detroit about the attack and hopped aboard a steamboat going north on Lake Huron. He got there two days after the shooting and took Albert Molitor to Detroit to get him the care he needed, but it wasn't enough. Molitor died on Sept. 18, at the age of 33, after spending his entire adult life subjecting the world to his greed and lechery.

Now, the law was duty-bound to find his killers and bring them to justice, even though he was pretty much unmourned outside his immediate family.

Sheriff John Rich assessed the scene of the crime, with the help of Larke, some Molitor cronies and other non-

MURDER WILL OUT.

Light at Last Thrown Upon a
Mystery of Sixteen Years Ago.

THE ASSASSINATION OF ALBERT MOL-
ITOR AND HIS CLERK.

William Repke's Conscience Wields a
Powerful Lash

THAT DRIVES HIM AT LAST TO MAKE
A FULL CONFESSION.

He Incriminates Sixteen Others in a Conspiracy to Murder.

WARRANTS ISSUED FOR THEIR ARREST—THE DARK
SECRET RECALLED.

(Detroit Free Press, Aug. 1, 1891)

criminologists. They could tell it was more than one killer, because they found different types of bullets and shot, fired from several different directions, and numerous sets of footprints facing the building.

They found one set of prints from a boot with a crooked heel. They knew that a man named Andrew Banks had a wonky heel and people asked him why he didn't get it fixed. They matched the boot to a print, perfect as Cinderella's slipper. But Banks said the boot was at the cobbler shop that night and he was visiting friends. The friends corroborated his alibi.

Any more clues or leads were hard to come by, and nobody seemed too eager to see the case solved.

And so, 16 years went by before anyone came forward.

In June 1891, William Repke's conscience had tortured him enough, and he'd blamed his unconfessed sin of murder for bringing illness and death to his children and livestock, fire to his home, and other slamming blows to his life.

"It was the sin what I keep them murderers in mine heart so long, I would clean mine heart," he said.

That turned a furrow on the cold case and brought up a lot of names, including Andrew Banks and Herman Hoeft. Banks had served as county treasurer under Molitor, and Hoeft, the stifled store owner, was said to be the mastermind behind the whole plot.

Two years later, and after a trial that caught the attention of the entire state, Repke was convicted along with three other foot soldiers and sentenced to life in prison. Repke was pardoned and released in 1901.

In the end, Repke gave 10 years of his own life as a balm for his guilt and as part of a town's token payment for the death of an unlamented tyrant.

DOWNSIZING CADILLAC

WHERE: FORT PONTCHARTRAIN (EARLY DETROIT)
WHEN: 1701–1710

ANTOINE DE LA MOTHE SIEUR DE CADILLAC IS A MOUTHFUL.

The founder of the fort that would grow into the city of Detroit was born Antoine Laumet, of humble background in southwestern France. He is a crucial chapter in the history of Detroit, but has also left a legacy of greed, and eventually, of contributing to the rise of slavery in the United States.

He gave himself the longer, fancier name to impress others with an implied air of nobility. In fact, sieur is French for sir or sire.

For quick reference, people now often refer to him simply as Cadillac, with no need for the rest of it. Yet that part was also an affectation. He added the name of a city near his hometown, to give his fake title a geographical focus.

Even his coat of arms—which would become part of the logo for the luxury car that would bear his name 200 years later—was made up, with trios of birds to signify the Holy Trinity and other more self-aggrandizing elements.

All of these falsehoods were just window-dressing, as he kept the lies coming, often to secure for himself greater and greater appointments from the crown of France, after he sailed to the New World in the early 1680s. He used those assignments mostly to achieve his real ambitions, which were to trade cheap brandy to Native Americans for their best furs, then send them to France for handsome profits.

We don't know exactly how Cadillac came to North America, but in 1683, he showed up in Acadia, then a part of New France, including areas that are now parts of Maine and Canada. Historians have not been able to find his name on any ship's manifest, so some have concluded he stowed away perhaps under an assumed name, or aboard an unregistered, possibly criminal, ship.

While in Acadia, Cadillac worked for privateers, which was a nicer word for pirates, working in the shadows for a particular European crown. Often, a town or colony hired privateers to attack their enemies' incoming cargo shipments.

Cadillac's village, Fort Pontchartrain, in 1701.

Fort Pontchartrain du Detroit is said to have been in the vicinity of where Larned and Griswold streets now meet, about a block north of where Hart Plaza sits.

While Cadillac privateered, he extensively explored that region of the eastern seaboard and proved himself valuable to French officials with his knowledge of the geography. On several visits to Quebec, he dazzled the governor general, the Comte de Frontenac, with his knowledge and charm. Frontenac appointed Cadillac in 1694 commander of Fort Michilimackinac in what is now Mackinaw City. As it was right where lakes Michigan and Huron meet, it was a strategic spot for the French to control, since several Native American tribes, as well as French and British trappers, traders and missionaries had to pass through the straits. Frontenac also wanted Cadillac to hold together the western Great Lakes tribes in an alliance against the British and their friends the Iroquois.

Yet, as usual, Cadillac was most interested in plying aboriginal people with liquor to get his hands on their animal pelts. He also underpaid the French fur-trappers, or coureurs de bois, for the pelts they provided him to be shipped to Europe. The wealthy people of Paris loved pelts from the New World, particularly beaver skins to be

used in hats. Other furs, as well, kept them warm and gaudily fashionable. The profits lined the pockets of Cadillac's long, wide-cuffed coats and kept him in the flowing wigs that he liked to wear.

People in Cadillac's orbit noticed how he shirked his official duties in order to make himself rich, but simply shook their heads at how those in power let it keep going. Louis Tantouin de la Touche, who led French troops at the fort, wrote of Cadillac: "Never has a man amassed so much wealth in so short a time and caused so much talk by the wrongs suffered by the individuals who advance funds to his sort of trading ventures," a stuffy and roundabout way of saying, "he's screwed over just about everybody."

Jesuit priests disliked him for providing booze to the weak-willed among the tribes, as they felt it made their job of converting Aboriginal souls more difficult.

Then, in 1697, a glut of furs in the French market started to cramp Cadillac's style. The king's representatives closed down several forts in response to the pelt industry recession, and decreed Michilimackinac a strictly military outpost, instead of one concerned with

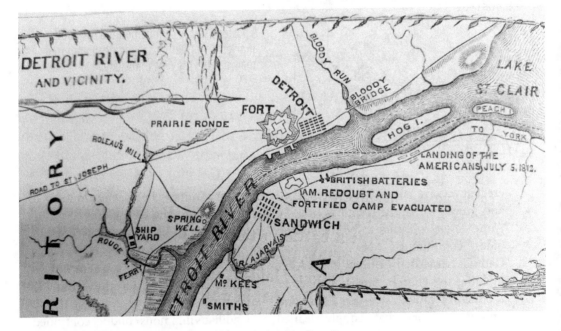

An early map shows Detroit's first gated community, Fort Detroit.

trading. That didn't appeal to Cadillac in the least.

While Michilimackinac was an important Great Lakes hub, Cadillac had his eye on a place that Europeans had not yet settled. He figured if he could establish a fort on the strait, or le détroit, between lakes Erie and St. Clair, he could better hold the British at bay, while gathering many tribes together to better exploit them. He sailed back to France and presented his case—a process that took a couple of years. He sold his idea to Jerome de Pontchartrain, King Louis XIV's minister of marine matters, as a way to convert Indigenous people to French ways, and to block the British and Iroquois from venturing further into the upper Great Lakes. He also appealed to the minister's vanity, as he planned to name the settlement Fort Pontchartrain du Detroit.

Cadillac's pitch succeeded and he sailed back to North America with royal approval. He then gathered about 100 soldiers and civilians and two priests in canoes along with supplies to set up shop in the pre-motor pre-city. They paddled north from Lake Erie to the point on the north shore that would become Detroit, Michigan, U.S.A. He chose the north side of the river because it would set him outside of New France (or what is now Canada), and give him a bit more freedom to run things in ways that would further profit himself. (It also set the stage for the future trivia question, "If you start in downtown Detroit and head due south, what is the first foreign country you reach?" Hint: not Cuba. In the future it would also make a local joke of the line in Journey's "Don't Stop Believin'" that goes, "...born and raised in south Detroit.")

Cadillac and his exploration party pulled up on the banks in the wilderness on July 24, 1701, and built a modest and crude wooden fort. The first building

A postage stamp commemorated the 250th anniversary of Detroit's founding, juxtaposed against a 1951 skyline of the city.

erected was a small church that endured and grew with the city, and is now St. Anne de Detroit, said to be the second oldest continuously operating Roman Catholic parish in the United States. After building the church, they put together a bunch of cabins with dirt floors and unhinged doors that simply leaned against the openings—uncomfortable lodgings even for that time and place.

Cadillac invited members of the French-friendly tribes of Huron, Wyandot, Miami, Odawa and others to camp out near the fort for trading purposes. He kept a shed well stocked with brandy to trade for furs, but made sure it stayed locked. He didn't want his own men getting drunk. Before too long, fort residents grew weary of the bad living conditions. His stinginess with the hooch and single-minded focus on his own profits made matters worse.

And when Cadillac left on a foray back to Quebec—a trip that included him being thrown in jail for a short stay due to bad reports about his leadership filtering back from "détroit"—he put in charge someone who made even himself look good in contrast. His substitute, Etienne Veniard de Bourgmont was a hot-head who started a needless war among the tribes (see page 11).

Eventually, word reached back to Pontchartrain in France, who was faced with the dilemma of removing Cadillac without admitting he'd been bamboozled into trusting the scoundrel. So, he reassigned Cadillac to the governorship of the Louisiana territory, which was the farthest reach of New France, so it received the least scrutiny from the crown.

Cadillac's infamous conduct continued there, as he failed to ingratiate himself to the southern tribes, and even refused to share the calumet, or peace pipe. He did help establish a lead mine in what is now Missouri, which the French appreciated at the time. But there's a dark historical cloud over that development, as the mine was an early importer of African slaves.

Now, while Fort Pontchartrain never really thrived under Cadillac's leadership, it did grow and achieve greater importance in the decades after his departure, first under the French, then under British rule and finally as a developing city when it became part of the United States.

After Cadillac retired from the Louisiana gig, he served time in the Bastille prison in France, possibly for insulting the king. Upon his release, he did receive honors from the French government, and retired to lead a comfortable life in the French countryside.

THE DOG THAT STARTED A WAR

WHEN: 1706
WHERE: FORT PONTCHARTRAIN (DETROIT)

ETIENNE DE VENIARD, SIEUR DE BOURGMONT IS LIKELY BETTER KNOWN IN MISSOURI AND THE GREAT PLAINS AREAS OF THE U.S. THAN HE IS IN MICHIGAN. That's because he mapped the Missouri and Platte rivers and studied the Native American tribes of that region.

Before he got to Missouri, however, he came through Michigan, got to be boss of the fort for a short stint, started a war among Indigenous tribes and then fled in disgrace.

Bourgmont's story started in Normandy, France. When he was 19, he faced either prison or a hefty fine for illegally hunting on the grounds of a monastery. Caught between the devil and the deep blue sea, he chose the sea, and sailed to North America. When he got there, he signed up as a French soldier and worked at a tannery where the Wabash River meets the Ohio River, until Cadillac summoned him up north to the fort. Somehow, the fort founder had enough faith in the young wanderer to leave him in charge of Pontchartrain while Cadillac went on a public-relations trip back to Montreal in 1706, to talk explorers and families into saying "oui" to Michigamme.

In March 1706, within weeks after taking the substitute post, things took a bad turn. For some reason, Bourgmont's dog—or a dog that belonged to the French fort—bit a young Odawa brave on the leg and the young man kicked the dog.

That unleashed the beast. Bourgmont hauled off and beat the young man. He pummeled and kicked him savagely, and the brave died a short time later.

The Odawa Indians, mourning the young man's death, figured someone had to pay, so they took it out on another tribe, the Miami, who were a favorite trading partner of the French. When the Odawa attacked, several Miamis fled into the fort to fight from within its walls. Soldiers fired from the fort and killed about 30 Odawa, and two of their own—a Catholic priest and a sergeant who hadn't gotten back inside the fort before the slugs began flying.

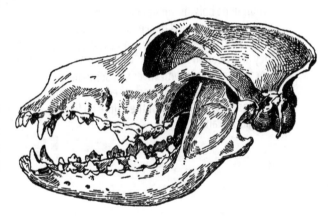

A coureur de bois, or "runner of the woods" is what they often called the French fur traders of the Great Lakes in the 1600s and 1700s. They also referred to them as "voyageurs" (not to be confused with voyeur, or someone who gets their kicks watching others in intimate acts), as they spent most of their time on long voyages by canoe.

After the musket smoke cleared and the fight ended, the Pontchartrain tenants placed the blame for the needless bloodshed where it belonged; on the shoulders of their hot-headed interim leader, Bourgmont.

Seeing the writing on the rough-hewn, wooden-log walls, Bourgmont abandoned his post and skipped town with two other Frenchmen. When Cadillac returned in August, he ordered the three hunted down and brought back to face punishment for desertion.

At first, Bourgmont took refuge among other deserters and illegal traders around Lake Erie, wandering between there and the Grand River valley. When Betellemy Pichon (one of the deserters) was captured, he covered for the others saying one had drowned and the other had been cannibalized by fellow French wanderers during a rough winter famine. Pichon was sentenced to be killed by having his head bashed in.

Despite his charge of desertion, and the possibility of having his own skull crushed in punishment, Bourgmont returned to the fort in 1712, and managed to avoid a gruesome penalty in part by helping fight a battle against the Fox tribe. Cadillac ultimately let the charges slide because Bourgmont's knowledge about the tribes of the area proved useful.

Because of this, Bourgmont lived to push his explorations further south and west and outlive the less than stellar reputation he'd made for himself in the fort at the straits.

CHIEF PONTIAC HEROISM AND CRUELTY

WHEN: MID-1700s
WHERE: FORT DETROIT, AND MORE

CHIEF PONTIAC'S NAME BECAME THAT OF A MICHIGAN CITY AND A GENERAL MOTORS CAR MAKE—TWO HONORS ALSO BESTOWED ON ANTOINE CADILLAC. PONTIAC IS ALSO KNOWN AS A RUTHLESS WARRIOR FOR A VALIANT, BUT LOSING CAUSE. Yet his legacy is marred by an act of cruelty to a child.

Chief Pontiac called together the Council of the Three Fires tribes to meet on April 27, 1763, at a bend in what the French called the River of the Barks, or Rivière Aux Échorches, now the Ecorse River. The Three Fires tribes are the Odawa (or Ottawa), Ojibwe (or Ojibway or Chippewa) and the Potawatomi. They hiked and paddled to the spot from areas that are now the rest of Michigan, northern Ohio and southern Ontario.

The throngs set up camp and listened to Pontiac make his case for an alliance to stop the British from taking their land and claiming personal ownership, not to mention for destroying their people and culture with alcohol, guns and diseases.

The relationship between the French and the tribes was far from perfect. Yet the fur traders had the good sense to participate in Indigenous customs, such as exchanging gifts and sharing the pipe. The French saw the Indigenous people as allies, and looked for compromises that would benefit both sides. Hey, that's just good business. On the other hand, the British who made it to that area were largely in the military. They saw the American Indians as inferior, and were more about forcing them to do their bidding, or getting rid of them altogether.

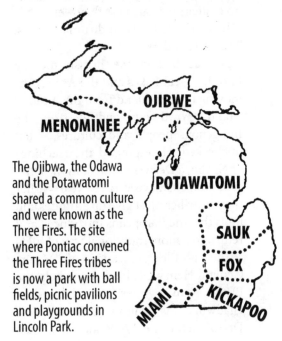

The Ojibwa, the Odawa and the Potawatomi shared a common culture and were known as the Three Fires. The site where Pontiac convened the Three Fires tribes is now a park with ball fields, picnic pavilions and playgrounds in Lincoln Park.

A depiction of dynamic Odawa Chief Pontiac, a brave and sometimes brutal fighter for his people and their culture.

To promote their supposed superiority, they refused to engage in tribal customs, no matter how harmless they were.

In short, the British didn't make deals. They gave orders.

Pontiac figured the British moving into the Great Lakes and the Americans moving further inland from the Atlantic would crowd out and destroy the Indigenous people and cultures, if left unchecked. He espoused the teachings of Neolin, a Delaware Indian in the Ohio area, who'd had a vision a few years earlier that the tribes must give up attitudes and tools that the Europeans introduced and return to a more traditional way of life.

The hostile demeanor of Major-General Henry Gladwin didn't help the British-Native American relationship. Gladwin was commander of Fort Detroit in the mid-1700s and considered

Indigenous people to be sub-human. He called them dogs to their faces, and when a tribe member gave him a gift, he broke it in front of him. When he executed a Native American woman, he left her body dangling on display for days. Gladwin is also said to have used the often-employed tactic of giving the tribal people blankets contaminated with smallpox and other germs.

In response, Pontiac assembled a force of 300 warriors to attack Fort Detroit. They entered the fort on May 7, 1763, with weapons concealed in their clothes. But someone had told Gladwin of Pontiac's plan, and 120 armed British men faced down Pontiac's party.

Pontiac retreated, but returned two days later and successfully laid siege to the fort. The attack killed several British civilians and soldiers who had ventured outside the fortress at that inopportune time. Pontiac's forces took several prisoners and ritually ate one of them. The chief also had some of the victims' bodies hacked into pieces and floated down the river past the British settlements, intending to break their spirits.

As the siege went on, with Pontiac's fighters surrounding the fort and controlling who could come and go, other tribe members joined Pontiac and their number grew to about 900. Three weeks into the siege, British reinforcements arrived to take down Pontiac. But the English were not ready for the stiff opposition of the Odawa leader and his fighters. He met them with a force of 400 men, outnumbering their 250 soldiers. It's become known as the Battle of Bloody Run, because the waters of Parents Creek ran red with the blood of the 20 British and seven of Pontiac's forces kiled in battle. Pontiac secured the win there, but the British in

Major General Henry Gladwin was commander of Fort Detroit, representing Great Britain, and made no secret of his contempt for Native Americans in his dealings with them. Gladwin County and city in Michigan are named for him. (Portrait by John Hall)

the fort continued to hang on, making it a waiting game.

Eventually, men fighting under Pontiac began leaving the stalemated blockade. They wanted to get back to their tribes and families and resume farming and hunting. In time, the siege fizzled and the Native Americans continued to lose ground.

Pontiac's resistance to the British earned him his heroic legacy. Yet there's a lesser known story that shows he may have been capable of astonishing cruelty.

It's said to have occurred while Pontiac and his people camped on the Maumee River, with French traders and a seven-year-old captive British girl. The Fischer family was among the early English farming clans in Detroit. After the deaths of her family members, Pontiac's tribe kidnapped the child. Betty Fischer

might have been raised as an Odawa, as other captives have been, had she not become sick with dysentery.

Now, it's understandable that Pontiac would see a deadly threat to his people in a European child with a serious intestinal illness. The mere presence of White people on the continent introduced new contagious diseases that killed up to 90 percent of the first inhabitants.

Yet it's still hard for many of us in the 21st Century to fathom Pontiac's rage when Betty Fischer soiled one of his blankets. He threw her into the Maumee. As she gasped to stay above the current and breathe, Pontiac ordered a nearby French trapper and trader to drown her. The man did as he was told.

Pontiac is said to have never admitted to or denied killing the girl. The British charged the Frenchman with murder. He disappeared before it came to trial. Pontiac was supposed to have testified at the trial, though the court proceeding never materialized. Later, the charges were dropped, as the British wanted to keep the peace with the tribes.

Pontiac eventually made his way to what is now Illinois. He met his end across the Mississippi River from the site that would become St. Louis when a member of the Peoria tribe snuck up behind him and clubbed him to death. Pontiac's murderer was after revenge, as Pontiac had stabbed the Peoria man's uncle. The uncle did not die from the stabbing, but he carried a grudge. Some have speculated that the British recruited the man to kill Pontiac, though that fact has never been substantiated.

EVICTING AN INCONVENIENT PEOPLE OR COL. PEPPER'S STONEY HEARTS CLUB BAND

WHEN: 1838
WHERE: ACROSS SOUTHERN MICHIGAN, BEGINNING NEAR SAGINAW

IN 1830, PRESIDENT ANDREW JACKSON SIGNED INTO LAW THE INDIAN REMOVAL ACT. That was seven years before Michigan became a state, when people were spreading the word about the territory's ripe-for-the-plucking timber, copper and iron ore.

As they did everywhere else in the U.S., the Europeans liked to buy up land in Michigan and sell its treasures on a grand scale. They felt the Indigenous people were in the way of their progress, and so they needed to be scooched over a few hundred miles. The federal government hired military officers to lead these removals and named Col. Abel C. Pepper as superintendent of the removal of Indians for Michigan, Indiana, Illinois and Wisconsin. The Ojibwe, Odawa and Potawatomi had to go.

Now, some tribes in Michigan had already suffered cataclysmic losses of their people through smallpox and other European diseases. The aliens from the east also liked to lay claim to land, seeing it as theirs to own and control, thereby nudging the tribes into smaller and more cramped areas.

In 1838, a year into statehood, the program kicked into gear in Michigan. It occurred the same year as the more infamous removal in southeastern states, spurred in part by discovery of a few flecks of gold in northern Georgia. The Cherokee were in the way of the White wave that arrived following the news of the gold. Soldiers began herding the people westward, removing them from much of the South. After convening in Tennessee, the soldiers marched the Native Americans by the thousand the rest of the way on the "Trail of Tears" to Oklahoma. Disease, hunger and depression claimed millions of the broken people in the Americas.

In Michigan, as the inevitable removal came nearer, some tribes tried to conform to White people's ways to stave off their ouster. The Pokagon Band of Potawatomi Indians, led by Leopold Pokagon, converted to Roman Catholicism and accepted land-ownership, buying land near

A Native American camp goes on in apparent peace and happiness as White settlements pop up nearby. Pretty soon though, the new neighbors want the old neighbors gone. (Sketch by a Baptist missionary)

what is now Dowagiac for the band. He fought stereotypes of Native Americans and abstained from alcohol at the Treaty of Chicago negotiations earlier in the decade, and so Pokagon's people were given the rare privilege of staying.

Another arm of the Potawatomi in the Saginaw Valley weren't given the same consideration that Pokagon's people received, however. People with more money than patience in Detroit and eastern U.S. cities were just starting to head from the depleted pineries of Maine to those in Michigan, and Saginaw was situated to become the city to control the wood's eastward flow. There were trees waiting to be felled, floated, sawed and sold on land that the Potawatomi occupied.

So, with President Martin Van Buren's blessing and Col. Pepper's direction,

troops on horseback trailed into the Saginaw River Valley and showed up at Potawatomi camps. The soldiers, under Pepper's orders, corralled man, woman and child, the sick, the old, everyone in the various camps and villages. Grab your things and follow us down the trail, they commanded. By force, they drove the area's first human inhabitants from the world that had sustained them and their ancestors for 12,000 years.

The first leg of the trip brought them to Owosso, a city named for Ojibwa leader Chief Wasso. Soldiers on horseback led several groups of the dispirited people from the Saginaw valley and other parts of southern Michigan, so that the military could assemble them into one group and escort them out of the state.

Chief Baw Beese, who led a band of Potawatomi near Hillsdale, was now part of a grim parade herded down dusty trails, through wooded hillsides, and down newly formed towns' main streets as the Europeans who had laid claim to the state stopped and watched.

The round-up brought Baw Beese and his people into the sights of future Democratic nominee for governor, Frederick Holloway. As Hollaway watched the people leave their land and freedom, he wrote this heart-rending—yet oddly nonchalant—description in his history of Hillsdale County:

> At the head of the column rode the aged chieftain in an open buggy, drawn by an Indian pony, alone, with his gun standing between his knees. A single infantry soldier, with musket on shoulder, preceded the buggy, while another marched on each flank. The chief had ceased to complain, but his countenance was dejected to the last degree as he drove in mournful silence away from the land of his forefathers.

He wrote of Baw Beese's wife and sons following, along with "a dozen more middle-aged and youngerly Indians and squaws, some on ponies and some on foot, and some of the squaws with papooses on their backs. These were probably the children and grandchildren of Baw Beese, and a special escort of a half a dozen soldiers was assigned to them."

Following the chief's family, the procession stretched about a half mile, Holloway continued:

> A few were on ponies but most of them on foot; stalwart warriors, with rifles on their shoulders but with mournful faces; women, still more dejected, with their blankets drawn over their heads; boys and girls, careless of the future, and full of mischievous tricks; and slung on their mothers' backs, the black-haired, bright-eyed, brown-faced papooses, the cutest-looking creatures in the world, gazing with infant wonder on the curious scene.

Despite his loving language toward some of the people passing by, Holloway seems callous to—or perhaps clueless of—the depth of the tragedy:

> The Indians were acquainted with almost every one, and as they recognized one and another of those who had been their friends, they called to them by name.
>
> "Good-by, good-by."
>
> "Good-by, good-by," responded the whites; and thus with friendly salutations the last of the Pottawattamies left for ever the home of their ancestors.

Holloway, by the way, lost the governor's election to one-termer David Jerome.

After the march through Michigan, the state's evicted Potowatomi people joined those of Indiana and other states, in a smaller version of the Trail of Tears. This one is often called the Potawatomi Trail of Death, as tragedies occurred all along the way.

Before the removal, some 400,000 Aboriginal people lived, died, hunted, farmed and traded in the state of Michigan. When the purge was done, that number had shrunk to 18,000. In other words, the new inhabitants let only four percent of the original residents remain within the borders of what the White people now called a state.

People of color were not admitted to the main section of the Fair, called the White City. Instead, they were invited to tour the exhibits of "authentic" villages from around the world, populated by real "natives." This may be where Simon Pokagon sold copies of his pamphlet. ("Official Views Of The World's Columbian Exposition: Dahomey Village—On The Midway")

As Leopold Pokagon had negotiated permission to have his band remain in Michigan, his son Simon Pokagon grew up in Michigan. Simon was a toddler at the time other Potawatomi were marched out of the state, and he took in the grief of his people that would only increase throughout his 69 years on the planet. He wrote about that loss and was sometimes called the "Red Man's Longfellow."

In 1893, the Chicago World's Fair—also known as the World's Columbian Exposition, to honor Christopher Columbus, whose landing on one of the Bahamas Islands 401 years prior set in motion the near extermination of Pokagon's race—was the talk of the modern world, as this young country flexed its expansionist muscle in a show of its greatest achievements. Simon Pokagon saw it from a completely different perspective.

Simon Pokagon wrote a reflection on the festivities in a 16-page pamphlet he titled Red Man's Rebuke, which he had letterpress printed on white birch tree bark. And so, in the city in which his father negotiated treaties 60 years earlier, Simon took copies to the World's Fair and sold them to White men in hats, high-buttoned coats and canes, and women in intestine-shuffling corseted dresses and wide, flowery hats. The pamphlet told of the centuries of cruelties Pokagon's people had suffered since Columbus' arrival. Yet, it's unclear whether the purchasers read it through or saw it as anything more than a quaint souvenir of a passing world.

Leopold Pokagon successfully negotiated permission for his band of Potawatomi to stay in Michigan, and adopted European religion and culture to help achieve that. His son, Simon Pokagon, wrote a pamphlet that he sold at the Chicago World's Fair in 1893, telling of the genocide of his people. Simon died six years later in a cabin in Michigan. (Painting of Leopold Pokagon, by Van Sanden)

Pokagon began the booklet like this:

On behalf of my people, the American Indians, I hereby declare to you, the pale-faced race that has usurped our lands and homes, that we have no spirit to celebrate with you the great Columbian Fair now being held in this Chicago city, the wonder of the world. No; sooner would we hold the high joy day over the graves of our departed than to celebrate our own funeral, the discovery of America. And while…your hearts in admiration rejoice over the beauty and grandeur of this young republic and you say, 'behold the wonders wrought by our children in this foreign land,' do not forget that this success has been at the sacrifice of our homes and a once happy race.

In a second printing, Pokagon changed the title to "Red Man's Greeting." The full text of the pamphlet is still available in several forms online, and you can even read it from photos of the original birch-bark edition at the Smithsonian Institution's web site.

Simon Pokagon was broke when he died six years later, in 1899, in a small cabin in Michigan. He was 69.

The Pokagon Band of Potawatomi gathers around a bonfire. Only 4 percent of the state's original human inhabitants were allowed to stay after U.S. troops marched them westward, a tragedy played out in many states. (Sketch of Kee waw nay Village by George Winter, 1837)

TANNER AND SCHOOLCRAFT: RELIGION, DECEIT AND MURDER

JOHN TANNER'S ROAD TO NORTHERN MICHIGAN STARTED IN TERROR WHEN HE WAS NINE YEARS OLD. His father was farming in the Ohio River Valley, near what is now Petersburg, Ky., when a band of Saginaw Ojibwa kidnapped him from home in 1789 and took him north.

His captors sold him to Netnokwa, a woman who led an Odawa band near the Straits of Mackinac. He learned hunting and trapping in his youth from the Odawa, trekking with them around the Lake Superior region to trap fur-bearing animals.

As an adult, he worked for a while on Mackinac Island, and dictated the story of his tumultuous life so far to Dr. Edwin James. When he took time off to visit a publisher in New York, he was fired. He relocated to Sault Ste. Marie.

He became valued in the Sault for his ability to interpret interactions between the two societies. One of those who used his services was the most famous and powerful White man in the town in the early 1800s, Henry Rowe Schoolcraft.

Schoolcraft studied Native American tribes in the upper Great Lakes from his office in Sault Ste. Marie. Schoolcraft was appointed in 1821 as the Federal

Agent to Indigenous People in the area and negotiated the treaty with the tribes in which they "ceded" much of what is now upper Michigan to the United States.

He's best known, however, for studying and writing about the customs, dress and culture of many of the region's tribes. He owes a lot of the credit to his wife, Jane Johnston Schoolcraft, half Ojibwa and half Irish, and a literary writer in her own right. She and her family arranged meetings between Schoolcraft and Native people. She also wrote down and translated a lot of the information for which her husband is known. Henry Wadsworth Longfellow used some of their ethnological writings in drafting his epic poem, "The Song of Hiawatha."

Schoolcraft needed a day-to-day translator and hired Tanner for that task.

While working together, the two men were often at odds. Both had tempers and Schoolcraft and the federal government were erratic with issuing Tanner his pay.

Eventually, Tanner had to borrow money and began going deeper in debt. Now, one of the big money-lenders in town just happened to be Schoolcraft's younger brother, James Schoolcraft. Dr. Edwin James believed the Schoolcraft siblings were working together to defraud Tanner.

When Schoolcraft finally fired Tanner, Tanner appealed to Gov. Lewis Cass, who asked Schoolcraft to keep him on and give him his back pay. Cass wrote of Tanner, "He seems to me a forlorn heart broken man." Schoolcraft refused.

Tanner took his anger out on his family, and a son ran away. He also lost his wife, though there are a couple different accounts of how that happened. In one version, Tanner had become jealous of soldiers at Fort Brady in the Sault, who were paying her too much attention for his liking. One day, after a disagreement, he stormed out of the house, ran into his runaway son and beat him bloody. Tanner was arrested and thrown in jail. His wife took that as an opportunity to leave on a boat bound for Detroit.

Tanner, however, claimed that he was walking down the street with her when soldiers came up and wrested her away from him. Tanner wrote of his version of the story in a letter he sent to President Martin Van Buren, complaining of that, his difficulty being paid, and his general grievances against Schoolcraft. He wrote that the Indian Agent had ruined his life.

As time went on, people in town were concerned about Tanner and his behavior, wondering about his mental health. He suffered headaches and convulsions, and lived near the fort, surviving on the vegetables he could raise on four acres in the Upper Peninsula's short growing season. He wished he could return to the Ohio River to be with his sister, but he couldn't afford the journey.

By the 1840s, he had gotten in trouble with the law twice for killing cows belonging to the Baptist Mission. He threatened Henry Schoolcraft and others.

In July, 1846, Tanner's house burned to the ground. On July 6, James Schoolcraft was shot at close range and killed. His body was found near his farmhouse, and on the same day, Tanner disappeared.

Considering John Tanner's untimely disappearance, his outstanding debts to James Schoolcraft, not to mention his animosities with Henry Rowe Schoolcraft, Tanner was the prime suspect, though evidence was slim and he was never charged.

A few years later, Tanner's body was found in a bog. The Schoolcraft killing remains unsolved.

LEAVE IT NO BEAVER
THE FUR-TRADING ERA

IN THE 1600s, THE FRENCH LEARNED THAT THE GREAT LAKES REGION HAD A WHOLE LOT OF BEAVERS, AND INDIGENOUS PEOPLE WILLING TO TRAP THE ANIMALS AND TRADE THEM. The furs made really nice felt hats, and because of that, had been trapped to near-extinction in Europe.

The French fur-trade era spanned about one hundred-thirty years, from the 1630s to the 1760s. The voyageurs, as the French traders were known, canoed and hiked around the Great Lakes, trading traps, axes, metal pots and eventually, guns, for skins of beaver, deer, otters, raccoons and other animals of the region. Their main posts of trade were the Mackinac Straits, Mackinac Island, Sault Ste. Marie and Fort Pontchartrain at the future site of Detroit, as well as Fort St. Joseph in what is now Niles. The French trekked all over the peninsulas, the voyageurs looking for furs to sell and the Catholic clergy looking for souls to convert.

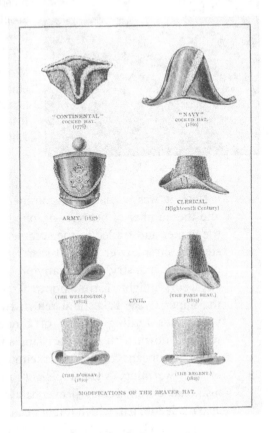

Beaver hat styles from 1776 to 1825.

Initially, the Huron tribe, in what are now Ontario in Canada and Michigan in the U.S., were known as particularly reliable traders. The Hurons obtained pelts from other tribes in exchange for grains and vegetables, then traded them in large quantities to the French. The era introduced the people of Paris to the lush furs of North American mammals and introduced the first Americans to metal tools. As mentioned in previous chapters, it also introduced diseases for which they had no immunity. Throughout the Americas, some estimate that smallpox, the flu and measles killed up to 90 percent of the Indigenous population in many areas.

It also reduced the numbers of several species in the region, particularly the beaver. About 10 million of the tree-gnawing, dam-building critters roamed the Great Lakes before White people arrived. Native Americans had trapped them for their own use, but on a much smaller scale.

THE ASTOR ERA - John Jacob Astor began to dominate the fur industry in the first part of the 19th Century. The German-born Astor married well and used his wife Sarah Todd's $300,000 dowry (about $6 million today) to start the American Fur Co. The dominance of the fur trade petered out about 1830, when the beaver population was pretty much played out. Still, Astor was believed to be the wealthiest person in America when he died in 1848.

Meanwhile, the Erie Canal brought Easterners here and other industries started flourishing. Pretty soon, the lumbering industry started up, and it was far more efficient than beavers in cutting down the state's trees. (Portrait of John Jacob Astor by Gilbert Stuart)

Now, it was a matter of commerce, and the number of beavers—trapped in the winter and traded in the summer—steadily shrank over the 130-year reign of the pelt industry. Particularly prolific voyageurs might leave Montreal for the upper Great Lakes and return two years later leading dozens of canoes weighed down with furs. Parisians and other Europeans couldn't get enough of the warming, water-repellant and fashionable animal coats. Beaver hair was also made into felt, which might become a top hat. Other parts of the animal were marketed through superstition, as beaver oil was said to improve memory and hearing.

By the 1690s, the traders were sending back more furs than the Europeans could buy or wear. Still, the government of King Louis XIV subsidized the North American fur trade in down times for political and strategic reasons. The animal-skin trade kept the French foothold in the Great Lakes and maintained valuable alliances with area tribes that strengthened Louis' position against the British.

The trade had consequences for the Indigenous population, beyond the diseases. The depletion of animals meant a depletion of meat and hide sources for the tribes. The metal tools for which they traded, and which became status symbols among them, made the people less self-reliant on their own handcrafted tools. The metal tools may have been more efficient, but the Native Americans lacked the means to reproduce them, so it increased their dependence on the Europeans.

When the British won the French and Indian War in 1763, and showed area tribes the rudeness and contempt that also offended Chief Pontiac, the animosity between the two groups grew. After the Revolutionary War ended with the Treaty of Paris, and Michigan became part of the territorial United States, the British were supposed to stop trading and doing business in the region after that. But since there was nobody enforcing the agreement, they remained in the area and kept up with business as usual, often acting as though they were still in charge. In fact, that's why we fought the War of 1812: to settle the matter once and for all.

FROM FURS TO FUDGE

The iconic Grand Hotel, known for having the world's longest porch, ushered in the island's resort period, just as the fur industry died out. The island was the hub of the fur highway, where French Canadian, Native American, British and U.S. pelt traders bought and sold animal skins.

The Anishinaabe named the island Mishimikinaak, or Great Turtle, for its turtle-like shape. Its strategic location for both commerce and armed forces, between lakes Michigan and Huron, operated under the French, British and then U.S. flags. In 1887, a conglomeration of railroad and shipping companies went in together and built the Grand Hotel, as they were already transporting a lot of tourists there.

The Grand has lived up to its name and played host to Mark Twain, John F. Kennedy and Madonna (not together). Actors Jane Seymour and Christopher Reeve misted up many an eye when they shot "Somewhere in Time" there in 1980.

HENRY FORD'S HENCHMAN

WHEN: 1920s–1945
WHERE: DEARBORN, FARWELL, YPSILANTI

HENRY FORD MET HIS MOST TRUSTED AND INFAMOUS CONFIDANT BECAUSE OF A NEW YORK CITY BRAWL.

Arthur Brisbane, a popular columnist for Hearst newspapers and outspoken opponent of Prohibition, watched the New York City street fight ignite that day in 1916. There was something impressive about the five-and-a-half foot tall Harry Bennett, his skills honed while boxing in the U.S. Navy and a lifetime of loving a good fistfight. His enthusiasm also caught the attention of the cops, who took him down to the nearest precinct to book him for his rowdiness.

Brisbane, who kept his ears to the gritty ground, learned that the sailor on leave with a mean jab and weave had roots in Ann Arbor. He also knew the Midwest magnate Ford was visiting the Big Apple at that time. He figured the arrested brawler Bennett needed his charges dropped and Ford undoubtedly needed muscle to intimidate dissatisfied wrench-turners, greedy ransom-seekers and any others who might pose a threat to Ford, his auto plants and his family. So, Brisbane arranged for the two to meet.

Thus began the long friendship between the two unlikely allies. Bennett joined the Ford Motor Company a year later when he left the Navy, and rose to head of security by the 1930s. Unimposing in stature, he nurtured a fearsome legend. Associates wondered about the pings they heard from his office, then found the favored new employee kept a pellet gun and would take a shot at a metal target at random times throughout his often stress-filled day. He also stashed a more lethal .45 in his office.

In conversation, he liked to drop names of gangsters like Chester "Chet" LaMare. LaMare was a mob boss who had provided the Ford Rouge Plant with vegetables as a front for his crime activity and was known as the "King of Hamtramck" before someone murdered him in his west-side home. In contrast to the thuggish image he cultivated, Bennett's wardrobe was more Harry Truman than Al Capone. Not that anyone was going to tell him to his face that bowties look a tad nerdy. He wore them because he wasn't going to wear a necktie that could become a noose if an enemy grabbed it.

Ford was fascinated with the tough young enforcer, and was known to leave early from his stodgier lunches with number-crunchers and sales execs so he could dart off to the security offices, where Bennett regaled his brawny lieutenants with tales of gangsters. Or sometimes, Bennett would fire up a projector and show grainy, black and white porn, at a time when such raunchy diversions were hard to come by.

Battle of the Overpass: A United Auto Workers drive for membership and better wages turned violent on this Miller Road overpass when Harry Bennett's team of strikebreakers showed up. (U.S. National Archives and Records Administration)

Yet what earned him his stripes with Henry was thwarting employees' efforts to unionize Ford plants at a time when General Motors and Chrysler were allowing labor unions a place at the table. He did this by ensuring that he and his minions infiltrated every area of the workers' lives. Ford moles posed as working stiffs at the blue-collar bars outside factory gates and kept their ears open for any talk of organizing. If someone stepped off the assembly line to relieve himself, he may just look over his shoulder to find a company rep following him into the bathroom to make sure he didn't pick up or drop off any subversive literature along the way.

Now, despite his resistance to organized labor, Ford had actually taken a historical step toward a living wage for his workers. In 1914 he raised wages to

at least $5 a day. That may not sound like much, but these days, it would be like almost $130 a day. It was a wage that allowed a family to eat well, buy a home and, more importantly to Ford, have enough left over to buy one of his cars. He did that early on, yet now he felt that the workers' requests for more were greedy attempts to squeeze more money out of his company. He felt that it was his place to decide their wages.

As laborers strove for more, things sometimes turned violent, and Bennett was often in the thick of it. One of those occasions was in the depths of the Great Depression. Ford's sales dropped and the company had to make massive lay-offs. Thousands had moved to Detroit, and now here they were, many hungry and without jobs or prospects. One icy March day in 1932, the laid-off workers

Future UAW president Walter Reuther, third from right, was hurt in the Battle of the Overpass when he was tossed down a couple flights of stairs for handing out pamphlets. (U.S. National Archives and Records Administration)

had had enough. More than 3,000 of them braved sub-freezing temperatures to march toward the Rouge Plant. As they got closer, fire hoses soaked them and pushed them back with tsunami-like force. Then came the guns. Police shot into the crowds. Bennett grabbed a protester to shield himself as the shots rang out, and the hapless fellow took a bullet for him.

Four protesters died that day from gunshots, another died later, and 22 suffered non-fatal injuries, including Bennett, who got hit by a rock.

The other clash that helped cement Bennett's legend as a fierce enforcer, doing Ford's bidding with goons and fisticuffs, is the May 26, 1937, Battle of the Overpass. United Auto Workers representatives, including future UAW president Walter Reuther, showed up at a footbridge over Miller Road, outside a Ford Rouge Plant gate, to hand out literature titled "Unionism, Not Fordism." They pushed for a shorter work day and a heftier paycheck, up from $6 to $8 a day for factory workers.

It started uneventfully enough for Detroit News photographer James Kilpatrick to lug his bulky camera over to the union reps to have them pose for a picture; no news photographer's preferred shot. The snaps he ended up getting were not staged at all. That's because right about then, 40 or so of his enforcers showed up to put an end to the pamphleteering. They weren't there to argue about it, either. They pulled one man's coat over his head to restrain him while they punched and kicked him.

They picked Reuther up and slammed him on the pavement several times, then dragged him to the steps and threw him down a couple flights of stairs. It was worse for union member Richard Merriweather. His attackers broke his back.

The union members suffered the worst physical injuries in the melee, but the car company's reputation received some serious scars, as well. When Bennett's bouncers ordered news photographer Kilpatrick to hand over the film from his camera, he gave them blank, unused film. With the rolls of damning images hidden under his car seat, he rushed back to the Detroit News and into the darkroom to develop the photos of the brawl. When the pictures ran in the paper, there was nothing Bennett could do to save the company's bruised public image.

Still, Ford valued Harry Bennett, perhaps above any other employee. He paid him handsomely enough for him to have two impressive homes, and some very exotic and dangerous pets. The turreted Geddes Road house on the Huron River, between Ann Arbor and Ypsilanti, known as Bennett's Castle, supposedly featured tunnels to where he kept pet lions and tigers. He entertained guests in tiled Roman baths and defended the picturesque grounds with a gun tower.

By many popular accounts, both of his homes reflected his mob-like persona and a life of opulent and paranoid excess. At his other home near the small town of Farwell, northwest of Clare, visitors spoke of an interrogation room with a single bench and steel hoops embedded in the wall, perhaps to shackle someone being questioned. The home had a swimming pool, and a bar with a window looking out to the underwater portion

A bloody Harry Bennett is helped up at the Ford Hunger March as he was hit by a rock that a protester threw at him. Bennett was hospitalized for the injury. It was first reported that he was shot. Five protesters were shot and killed in the confrontation. (The South Bend Tribune, June 8, 1937)

of the pool, so he and male guests could have a lecher's-eye view, underwater, of women swimming in the pool. A feature of both homes was uneven stairways. Bennett would run up and down them to memorize the idiosyncrasies that would likely send a pursuer into a tumble of pain and broken bones.

Ford confided in Bennett his personal matters, as well as business concerns. Biographers have speculated that Bennett helped the big boss cover for a mistress and an out-of-wedlock son. Oh, and further spicing up the scandal, the mistress was married to another of Ford's trusted assistants, a guy who worked under Bennett.

Harry Bennett, left, speaks with attorney George Burke, as Bennett agreed to speak before a grand jury regarding the Battle of the Overpass. Bennett wasn't with his enforcers when the confrontation began, but witnesses said it was the anti-union forces that started the violence, just as some of the demonstrators were posing for a news photo. (The South Bend Tribune, June 8, 1937)

Ford's close relationship with Bennett often overshadowed his relationship with his family, and some of the Fords resented it. They felt Henry valued Bennett's opinion over that of his son Edsel, who had actually been named president of the company, though Henry frequently went against his decisions. Edsel's son, Henry Ford II, was to take over if anything happened to Edsel. Yet when Edsel died in 1943, Hank the Deuce, as he was sometimes known, was fighting in World War II. So, an aging and increasingly erratic Henry—the original model—became president again for a couple of years.

When Hank the Deuce returned from military service, he squared off with his grandfather on several issues, and his disapproval of Bennett's tactics topped that list. He voiced his concerns to board members about the dark and violent image that was overtaking the company at the hands of Bennett, not to mention that his grandfather had a well-known history of anti-Jewish sentiments (see page 32), that put the company in a worse light than ever after the U.S. had fought Hitler.

Young Henry wanted to replace his grandfather at the helm and take the automaker into a more modern and publicity-conscious direction. And he wanted Bennett out. He had to broach that topic carefully, and pull strings behind the scenes, since everyone knew of the company founder's infatuation with the Bow-Tied One. The women in the family also got into the act, generally taking young Henry's side. It was his mother Eleanor, Edsel's widow, who helped turn the old man in the end, when she threatened to sell her 41 percent of the company's stock if he didn't put his grandson in charge. He relented and made his name-sake president of Ford Motor Company in September, 1945.

HF2's first order of business, of course, was to fire Bennett. He gave John Bugas, another pugilist in a suit, the task of delivering the unpleasant news. Bugas had sharpened his own tough-guy credentials in the FBI's Detroit office, dealing with some of Bennett's underground friends. Ironically, Bennett had brought Bugas aboard to keep him close after Bugas had investigated embezzlement from the company, and Bennett feared him fingering some of his favorite employees.

As Bugas prepared to tell Bennett that he was fired, he anticipated resistance and tucked a .38 into his belt. When he showed up in the doorway of Bennett's office, Bennett stood up and yelled, "You son of a bitch!" He pulled a .45 out of a desk drawer and pointed it at Bugas.

Bugas warned him not to pull the trigger.

"I'll put one right through your heart, Harry," he said.

Despite the tension of the show-down, this was not the OK Corral and no shots were fired. Bugas walked away to tell the new company president that the deed was done. Bennett stayed until the end of the day, filling the halls with the smoke of burning files he didn't want to leave behind. Then he left the building and Ford Motor Co. for good.

He probably didn't have much of a future there anyway. Henry Ford, the founder of the company who had been so impressed with Bennett the young brawler three decades before, died less than two years later.

HENRY FORD, AND THE THIRD REICH'S SEAL OF APPROVAL

WHEN: 1919–1927
WHERE: DEARBORN, AND AUTO SHOWROOMS ALL OVER THE COUNTRY

WALK INTO A CAR DEALERSHIP SHOWROOM AND SEE WHAT KIND OF READING MATERIAL YOU FIND. Glossy brochures of cars are just about it, outside the People, Golf Digest and local newspaper in the service waiting room.

Dial back to the days when you might stroll on down to the Main Street Ford dealer to look at the new Model T touring cars and runabouts. While you wait for a salesman, you glance at the coffee table and spot the latest copy of the Dearborn Independent, with the headline: "The Jewish Question: Fact or Fancy" for an article that went on about "world-controlling Jews." That wasn't an unusual headline, either, for the newspaper that Henry Ford provided to and pushed onto Ford dealership owners. From 1919 to 1927, the paper frequently ran essays promoting Ford's prejudices, such as his opinion that Jewish bankers encouraged the start of World War I in order to make money.

Without Ford, both Michigan and the world's industry, transportation and labor would be much different today. Yet, in addition to changing the world with the assembly line and initially helping to promote a living wage in order to sell his cars, Ford had some well-known and troubling personality traits.

Chief among the skeletons that many have wanted to put in the closet since his death was his virulent antisemitism, even though he made no secret of his prejudices. He shared his world view in essays and around campfires with the likes of lightbulb magnate Thomas Edison, tire tycoon Harvey Firestone and President Warren G. Harding.

On those camping trips, which Ford organized, Jews weren't the only ones he blamed for society's ills. He pontificated on many supposed scourges of the day, like the ever-shortening length of women's skirts, and that loud, unruly jazz music. In fact, he blamed Jews for the rise of jazz, thereby

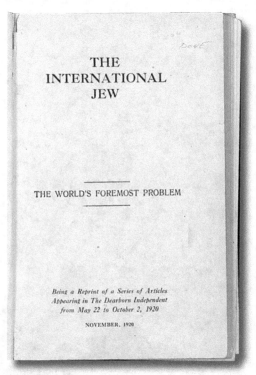

Henry Ford and "The International Jew" a reprinting of anti-semitic essays from Ford's Dearborn Independent newspaper. The reprints traveled around the world and made several fans among the Nazis. (1919 portrait of Henry Ford by Hartsook)

negating a cultural achievement of the African Americans, while offering one more reason to resent the Jewish people.

The opportunity to spread his views to a wider audience came as the owners of the Dearborn Independent were struggling to keep the weekly newspaper afloat. The paper was covering the town, which was still mostly rural, but that wasn't paying its bills. Ford bought the operation for $1,000, which is still the equivalent of only $15,000. Not a bad price for the means to amplify his political voice.

Ford didn't actually write the articles, though. He hired writers and editors—some of them also vehemently antisemitic—to produce content tailored to his own opinions. He even had people spy on some influential Jews around the country to provide fodder for the printed invective.

The published diatribes continued until Aaron Sapiro, a lawyer and a farmers' movement organizer, sued the paper for stating that Jews were provoking violence. The article that led to the suit named Sapiro and several other Jewish leaders as the supposed troublemakers. Editor William Cameron swore that Ford was not the source of the content, but others said Ford had absolute control over what was written.

The suit got Henry Ford's attention. In July, 1927, he asked Louis Marshall, who was a lawyer and a Jewish activist, to write an apology letter for him to sign. Marshall actually did so, apparently just

In 1913, Henry Ford instituted the moving assembly line at the new Highland Park plant, which sped up production of the Model T and brought down the price, making it the first car for the average Joe and Josephine. Assembly lines have been adapted to many manufacturing industries, as well as fast food, which is as inseperable from automobile culture as dried ketchup and secret sauce are from many a driver's seat.

wanting to see an end to the ugliness, and perhaps he believed Ford's contrition. Not surprisingly, Marshall received a lot of criticism for helping Ford cover up his sins. Still, it seemed to have worked. Sapiro ended up dropping the lawsuit.

Now, it takes a strong person to stand up to a mistake and carry the blame on one's own shoulders. Henry Ford was not that person. In his written apology, he claimed he hadn't known what his underlings at the Independent were

writing and, by gum, they'd better stop it.

"Ford was satisfied that those whom he had put in charge of the Dearborn Independent had taken advantage of him by publishing a series of articles attacking Jews," Louis Marshall wrote in the letter directed at the plaintiffs, and generally to all who had taken offense with Ford's opinions.

Still, the damage of toxic ideas was done. Ford's underlings had already

Nazi Germany so appreciated the anti-semitic writings Henry Ford published that officials awarded the auto magnate the Grand Cross of the German Eagle. Other recipients included Charles Lindbergh, aviation hero and Detroit native who espoused similar views to Ford's; Nazi leader Heinrich Himmler, who developed the dreaded SS paramilitary force and the concentration camps; and Italian dictator Benito Mussolini.

reprinted many of the writings in a book series titled The International Jew. A young, relatively unknown Adolf Hitler loved the stuff and had a picture of ol' Hank in his office. The future Fuhrer even gave Ford a shout-out in his own book, Mein Kampf. And later, the Nazi party handed out copies of The International Jew to win Germans over and get them to hate the same people Hitler and his boys hated. In 1938, the Nazis awarded Ford with the Grand Cross of the German Eagle, a golden beaut dangling on a red ribbon, festooned with Roman eagles and four swastikas.

The original Henry didn't stick around forever, and when the shareholders passed the torch to his grandson, Henry Ford II, aka Hank the Deuce, he spent decades reaching out to minorities and trying to undo the damage his talented but tainted grandfather had done to his own creation.

The city of Dearborn, however, tried to put that skeleton right back in the closet in 2019, when veteran journalist Bill McGraw wrote a piece for The Dearborn Historian magazine, which examined Ford's legacy of hate. The city owns the publication and the mayor had the story killed when he caught wind of it. He fired McGraw, as well. The effort to silence the story backfired, however, as censorship often does. In fact, it put the whole issue into heavy rotation in media and social media for a while. When public outrage reached the mayor's office, he backpedaled, and released the article in different packaging.

McGraw's piece tells the history of Ford's writings, but also highlights their influence on hate groups today, naming Nazi and white supremacist Web sites that have carried Ford's messages.

McGraw puts it in historical perspective. "Ford's salvos were likely the most sustained printed attacks on Jews the world had ever seen," he wrote. "With his wealth and resources, Ford remains the most formidable anti-Semite in American history."

MAGNATE MAP

Henry Ford is everywhere in Dearborn. His last name sits atop the company's world headquarters building, commanding its stretch of Michigan Avenue, in a huge version of the familiar blue oval on Ford cars and trucks. About five miles southeast of there is the sprawling Rouge Plant, which took 11 years to build and was the largest factory in the world when it opened in 1928. At one time, it housed just about every aspect of car manufacturing, all in one complex. Hundreds of thousands of school kids took field trips there to see the orange molten steel at the beginning of the assembly line, and shiny, new Mustangs and other glistening Fords coming off at the end, where drivers hopped in and parked them in a huge lot, waiting to be trucked out to the dealers.

The plant takes its name from the Rouge River, which winds behind the plant, and into which the several factories and refineries pumped industrial waste for decades. In October, 1969, a worker dropped a torch, which lit the river on fire where oil had spilled from a Shell storage site. Flames climbed 60 feet. In the 50 years since, concerted efforts and restrictions have cleaned it up considerably.

Then there's Greenfield Village and the Henry Ford Museum. They now refer to the entire complex as the Henry Ford. The Village is a nostalgic collection of old-time Americana and historical buildings, like the Wright Brothers' bicycle shop, Thomas Edison's workshop and the shed in which Henry built his first car. The Henry Ford Museum of American Innovation chronicles mechanical and technological progress through cars, trains, planes and appliances. It has the chair in which Lincoln was shot, and the Montgomery, Ala., bus in which Rosa Parks refused to stand. Parks moved to Detroit in the late 1950s, and remained politically active. She died in 2005 and is buried in Woodlawn Cemetery on Woodward Avenue between 7 and 8 Mile roads.

Fair Lane, the 31,000-square-foot mansion of Henry and his wife Clara Ford, sits buffered from the bustle of Dearborn on 1,300 acres along the Rouge River—upriver from the factory, of course. As of this writing, crews are renovating the home, and the grounds are open for visitors at certain times.

Outside of Dearborn, on Woodward Avenue, is Ford Motor Company's very first auto plant, the Highland Park Plant, in the city of the same name. It's the assembly plant that ushered in the Model T, the $5 work day, and thereby, the blossoming middle class of the 20th Century. The building stands idle in Highland Park, which is one of two suburbs completely surrounded by the city of Detroit. The other is Hamtramck.

The Fair Lane mansion.

FORD RETIRES TO HIS $100,000 HILL COTTAGE, 'NOTHING TO SAY'

(Santa Rosa Republican, Sept. 1, 1933)

(Copyright 1933 by United Press)

MARQUETTE, Mich., Sept. 1 (UP)—Henry Ford clung to the fastness of his Huron Mountain Club retreat today as the government's drive to bring him under the NRA made itself felt here.

The famous automobile manufacturer's position on the Roosevelt recovery program was the subject of most of the conversation on the streets, in lodges and clubs and summer homes here. Opinion was divided as to his future course. Some intimate friends quoted him as talking vehemently in opposition to the Recovery Act and calling it "unfair competition."

Forty miles up the rugged coast

THE CLUB TOO RICH FOR HENRY FORD

Northwest of Marquette, the hump on the map of the U.P. just east of the Keweenaw Peninsula, is a rugged paradise for outdoor lovers. The entire area is known for its relatively unspoiled condition. Yet there is one area that is particularly untouched, and that's because, well, most of us aren't welcome there.

The Huron Mountain Club is a 20,000-acre sanctuary for old-growth forest, the bald eagle and the industrial American aristocrat. It covers about one-fifth as much land as the city of Detroit.

The founders of Miller Brewing and International Harvester tractors were among those who bought up land in the area in the late 1800s. When landholders pooled their tracts and established the exclusive club, they capped inclusion at 50 members and 100 associate members.

In the late 1920s, Henry Ford wanted into the exclusive club, but Ford wasn't really the kind of people they were looking for.

Yes, the man who put America on wheels and was, because of it, the eighth richest person in the world, didn't have the right stuff to bypass the waiting list and get into the Huron Mountain Club. He could have waited for someone to die or leave the club and then hope he would rise to the top of that list. But still, some of the members weren't sure they wanted someone like Ford, who had controversial views and was constantly in the news. Would he blab about the club and destroy its privacy and mystique? See, like "Fight Club," the members of Huron Mountain Club don't talk about it.

But Ford saw an opportunity. The club members were petrified that a state road, M-35, was going to bulldoze and pave a strip right through their paradise, as the blueprints showed it doing. It would have, except that in 1927, Henry Ford did some land shopping in that area and snapped up several parcels that stood in the road's way. Though the engineers had mapped the road before Ford ever even thought of buying the land, the state didn't want to barge in on its best-known citizen of the day. Thus, Ford scratched the backs of the club members and they opened the guarded gates to him in 1929. He had a $100,000 ($1.4 million now) "cabin" built on the property.

Nobody has ever admitted or elaborated on how Ford got into the close-lipped club. But it's fairly apparent once you follow the money. And the road.

YOU MAY WANT TO DODGE THESE BROTHERS

WHERE: DETROIT
WHEN: 1910ISH – 1920

OF DOZENS OF MACHINISTS AND DREAMERS WHO TRIED THEIR HANDS AT BUILDING AND SELLING CARS, JUST A FEW HAVE MADE IT TO SOME SORT OF IMMORTALITY. Ford, of course, leads the pack, but keeps company with Chrysler, Chevrolet, Olds, Buick and Dodge, as those whose names have also been immortalized on automotive nameplates. Several of them have staid images as talented engineers or astute business leaders—or as a racer like Louis Chevrolet—with fewer saucy stories available about them.

Not so for the Dodge brothers.

John Francis Dodge and Horace Elgin Dodge gained reputations for heavy drinking and bullying, along with their well-deserved laurels in the business world. In the Dodge partnership, John was an outgoing businessman, and Horace a gifted machinist who preferred to work behind the scenes, where he didn't have to suffer the company of strangers. Each one liked his liquor and flexed his fists freely when someone crossed him.

The pudgy-faced, red-headed brothers grew up the sons of a riverboat-engine builder in Niles, on the St. Joseph River and just this side of the Indiana border. While growing up, their family struggled because, by the time their father took over the boat-engine trade from his father, trains were rapidly replacing riverboats in moving people and freight around the country. A search for a better living eventually led the family to move from Niles to Port Huron, and later to Detroit.

Despite those struggles, John and Horace followed their father into mechanical-related careers. Unlike him, however, they had the sense or the luck to ultimately find their way into the new and growing field of automobiles, rather than the fading world of riverboats.

When the two brothers became adults, they learned machining and mechanical skills at a series of jobs, before partnering with Frederick Evans in 1896 to make Evans and Dodge Bicycles in Windsor, Ontario. Horace demonstrated his talent in design and machining by inventing and patenting a ball bearing system that resisted dust and dirt, solving the problem of wheel mechanisms clogging and stopping up.

In 1901, the brothers opened their own machine shop in Detroit, with Horace tending to the mechanical end and John running the business end.

DODGE BROTHERS' NEW AUTOMOBILE PARTS MANUFACTORY

One of the Finest of Its Kind in This Country and Which is Now Ready to Make Its Debut to the Automobile World

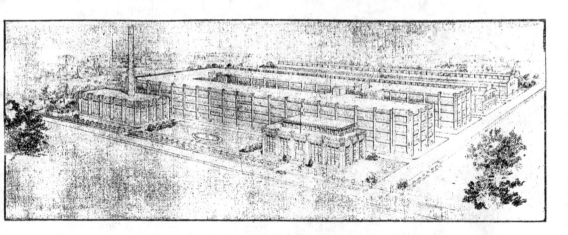

John and Horace Dodge had this factory built in Hamtramck to prodtuce auto parts, as they were a major parts provider to Ford Motor Co. Before the decade was out, they were making and selling Dodge cars. That threw a wrench into the Dodge brothers' already sputtering relationship with Henry Ford, a relationship that may have pushed the hard-drinking, surly brothers into harder drinking and extra surliness. (Detroit Free Press, Jan. 15, 1911)

At first, they made stove parts. (Detroit, incidentally, was known for making stoves before motors took over. However, nobody is known to have coined the tag Stotown.) They eventually branched out into car parts, making engines and other components for Ford Motor Co. and Olds Motor Works. With heavy-hitting customers like that they opened a much larger plant in Hamtramck in 1910.

Four years later, they rolled out the first automobiles bearing the Dodge nameplate. Horace once again proved his talents with several new innovations, including a method to bake enamel onto auto bodies.

The Dodges already had a strained relationship with Henry Ford, and it really ground Ford's gears to have his contractors now producing entire cars to compete with his. The Dodges, on the other hand, weren't crazy about the fact that Ford paid them with company stock, even though they eventually sold the stock back to him for $25 million (equal to about $370 million today) after Henry stopped paying dividends on their shares and they sued him.

Some say that working with the Dodges gave Henry Ford one more prejudice to add to his list of biases: redheads. It's said that after the Dodges, Ford was paranoid about hiring or contracting with anyone who had red hair.

On their part, it's said that Ford drove the Dodges to drink. Even more than already, that is. John and Horace were often seen tossing back drinks together, wearing identically tailored suits.

39

Louis Chevrolet provided the name to one of the best-known car brands. Chevrolet was a race-car driver, hence the leather cap and goggles, who started Chevrolet Motors with William C. Durant. Chevrolet left within a few years and started Frontenac Motors to build racing parts for Model Ts. Durant kept the swiss racer's name for his company, and eventually built General Motors, which would include Cadillac, Oldsmobile, Buick and other brand names and would become the largest company in the world in the mid-1900s. (General Motors publicity photo)

When they fought with each other, it could get loud, and those around them at those times, kept their distance.

But it was their fights with others that gave them a reputation for being dangerously volatile. John once pulled out a revolver and made a bartender dance on the counter, then threw glasses at the mirror in applause. Horace beat a man unconscious for making fun of him when he couldn't crank-start a car.

In 1911, the Detroit Times reported that John and a friend badly beat a handicapped lawyer in a brawl at Schneider's Bar. John threatened to kill the owner of the newspaper and the lawyer filed a suit, which he later dropped.

On the social front, their well-known drunken rowdiness hindered their efforts to enter the elite inner-circles of Detroit and Grosse Pointe. The aristocrats couldn't be connected to such low-brow antics.

Yet by and by, Horace and his musician wife Anna did what they could to overcome the brothers' personality deficits. The couple was actually beginning to make inroads into high society by helping to fund the Detroit Symphony Orchestra. They were also leaders in building Orchestra Hall, which is renowned for its acoustics and is once again the home of the orchestra following extensive renovations earlier this century.

People come and go outside the Dodge Brothers storefront in the 1920s or '30s.
(Matson Collection, Library of Congress)

Whatever progress they made in being accepted by the upper echelon, they didn't have long to enjoy it. In January, 1920, after they attended an auto show in New York City, Horace caught pneumonia. John sat at his bedside, became ill himself and died within 10 days.

Horace was distraught at his brother's death and, in the last month of the same year, his drinking caught up with him and he died of cirrhosis of the liver. John was 55 and Horace 52.

By the time of their deaths, they had built their car brand into the third best-selling automobile in America, and they couldn't build them fast enough to satisfy demand.

The company lived on as a name plate for parent company Chrysler, which bought Dodge in 1928. Dodge is still a popular brand for Chrysler, though some have speculated that it would have reached even greater heights if the brilliant—but bizarre—Dodges had lived longer.

CLEANERS AND DYERS WAR

WHERE: DETROIT
WHEN: 1920s

DYNAMITE, STINK BOMBS AND BULLET-RIDDLED CORPSES PUNCTUATED A WAR IN 1920s DETROIT. This war had nothing to do with illegal liquor, as did other bloody, underground conflicts of the jazz decade. This war was about cleaning and dyeing cloth and throughout it ran the red of blood and the hue of the city's growing menace known as the Purple Gang.

It all started with a price war. The Motor City had dozens of cleaning and dyeing businesses, and with such fierce competition, they had to keep their fees painfully low. However, no matter how low they marked down their fees, another shop always came along and undercut them. On top of that, tailors and others who used the shops in large volume often declined to pay their bills. They didn't have to worry about a stiffed cleaner refusing their future business. They could just take their linens to another of the shops that was glutting the city's market. Virtually everybody in the cleaning and dyeing business lost money.

If only the shop owners had banded together to agree on a price structure that would cover their costs. Then, maybe, they could all profit. Francis X. Martel, representing the Detroit Federation of Labor, recruited Ben Abrams, a labor leader from Chicago with experience in starting up such an association.

Abrams hired Charles Jacoby, Jr., an in-law of the vicious Bernstein brothers who led the Purple Gang, Detroit's most notorious and powerful organized crime gang in the '20s, to be president of the new Wholesale Cleaners and Dyers Association. He owned a shop himself, but his main asset was his relationship to the Bernstein brothers.

The new association recruited effectively. Its representatives told shop owners they were there to help solve their money woes. Problem is, they pledged allegiance not to the people who cleaned and dyed the cloth, but rather to the Purple Gang. Through Jacoby's link, the lavender league served to collect dues—in other words, they shook down the cleaning shops for hefty membership dues—and to, ahem, enforce the association's will. See, the association did offer a type of protection to its members. It protected the business owners from their protectors.

In a nutshell, the association or union or whatever you want to call it, was a front for gangsters. The Purple Gang made hundreds of thousands of dollars in collecting dues at whatever price they deemed fair.

MODERN CLEANING AND DYEING PLANT TO BE OPENED BY JACOBY'S TODAY

(Detroit Free Press, Oct. 11, 1925)

The Wholesale Cleaners and Dyers Association collected from members to buy two plants that all members could use, but they blew up soon after the money was raised.

Don't want to join? The proprietor might arrive one morning to find a stick of TNT with a half-burnt wick waiting at the doorstep. A message like that could be quite persuasive.

Not paying your dues? A "stench-bomb", as they called them, just might go off inside your shop. This kind of bomb doesn't blow up your building. It just fills the air inside with an unbearable odor that settles into everything, and particularly cloth. All the linens sent by your customers now stink to high heaven and are rendered worse than worthless. The customer loses money and you lose the customer. Sometimes, the mobsters ruined clothes with a phosphorous solution that ignited in a warm room. Several shops suffered, or were outright destroyed, by such targeted vandalism.

Want to speak out against this injustice or oppose it in any way? Go ahead. That's admirable and takes real guts. But speaking of guts, yours just might end up ripped open by a hitman's bullets.

Sam Sigman and Samuel Polakoff were two shop owners who tried. They openly defied the mob's authority by jacking up their fees. Both were eventually found dead, riddled with bullets. Sigman's body

43

painted the snow with the blood oozing out of several bullet holes on a roadside on Dec. 9, 1926. Samuel Polakoff of Union Cleaners and Dyers stained the back seat of his own car with two bullets in his head, and one each in his chest and leg, before his body was found in his car at the corner of Dexter Boulevard and Grand Avenue on March 22, 1928.

And that's how the Cleaners and Dyers War played out for three years. The Purples lurked in the shadows of the trade association that was supposed to help its members.

The gang also squeezed from its members to help build two large shops, a project that they said would work for everyone. The theory was that those cooperative shops would process clothes for smaller businesses, which would cut their costs. In this way, the union, er, mob, collected hundreds of thousands of dollars to buy two buildings, then both buildings blew up in fiery nighttime blasts, ending the "project." No refunds for the investors.

The good news is that some of the cops and the prosecutors were watching and compiling a case and in 1928, Wayne County Prosecutor Robert Toms charged 13 men with conspiracy to extort the cleaning-and-dyeing mom and pops. Abe and Ray Bernstein were also charged, along with several lower-profile members of the Purple Gang.

The trial laid bare how they conducted business. Jacoby, one of those charged, took the stand and said he had left the group after paying $18,000 in dues (about $260,000 today) over three years. When he got fed up and left the organization, he and his wife received menacing phone calls at home. The phone rang, he or she picked it up and said "Hello," and a man's voice said, "Get in line," and then hung up.

He didn't get in line, but saw his shop turn victim to theft, stench-bombing and arson.

Prosecutor Toms showed how the gang used association dues to fund bootlegging and to pay the hitman who murdered their enemies, including cops who couldn't be paid off to look the other way.

Toms detailed stories of stench-bombings, dynamitings, and corpses of dissenters.

And Toms' star witness, Harry Rosman, showed several cancelled checks of $500 to $1,000 when he and his shop had to pay the regular dues and also extra charges at the gang's whim. When they wanted extra cash, like to buy the two buildings for the cooperative shop, they told him to not ask any questions.

Somehow, Rosman lived another 30 years after his brave testimony. Maybe that's because it didn't really lead to any convictions.

In the end, in fact, all suspects were acquitted, perhaps due to jurors feeling intimidated by the defendants tossing menacing glances their way throughout the trial.

Still, the packed courtroom spectacle brought an end to the war, and to the Wholesale Cleaners and Dyers Association.

The Purples had bigger fish to fry, anyway. They emerged from the highly publicized hearings as the most powerful criminal enterprise in a city awash in bootlegging, gang rivalries and gruesome mob hits. They would go on to reign for three more bloody years. That is, until an overreaching hit known as the Collingwood Estate Massacre led to the arrests of their top brass, and another trial that weakened the gang enough for others to hop in and fill the void.

Above: A few years after the Cleaners and Dyers War, the Collingwood Massacre perpetrated by the Purple Gang drew a crowd outside the scene of the crime.

Below: Joe Bernstein, second from left, and other defendants are charged in the Collingwood Massacre, which would damage the Purple Gang in ways the Cleaners and Dyers War trial failed to do.

THE HONEYMOON IS OVER

WHERE: FLINT & TOLEDO, OHIO
WHEN: 1980

FRED TUCKER, A FORMER FLINT CITY COUNCILMAN, WAS REMARRIED ON THE DAY HIS EX-WIFE EVELYN DIED FROM A LENGTHY ILLNESS. Fred and Evelyn had remained amiable after the divorce, so friends were surprised when the newlyweds failed to show up at her funeral. In fact, nobody saw them anywhere. Tucker and his new bride, Louise Caston, had disappeared.

Three days later, on Dec. 19, 1980—just a week after their marriage—their bodies were found in Ohio.

That left Tucker's neighbors and constituents on the north side of Flint wondering why this would happen. Tucker had been a popular councilman, reputed to know how to get things done for his constituents. That also made him some enemies, as his deftness in manipulating people may at times have come at someone else's expense. He was said to often have had a gun stuffed into his waistband. Still, when he'd recently resigned from the council, he did so having never lost an election in his 11 years of city politics. Relatives said he had hoped to run for mayor of Flint within a couple years or so.

On the other hand, Tucker's career in hospital administration hadn't ended so well. A couple years earlier, he'd resigned as head of Mercy Hospital in Flint with a cloud over his head. He was accused of using the institution's employees and materials to fix up some of his investment properties around town. Federal agents investigated him on the accusations, but never indicted him over the apparent improprieties. Still, that's likely what led to him leaving his position at Mercy to focus full-time on his real-estate business.

In fact, it was at his real estate office on the north side of Flint that he and Louise were last seen alive. That was about midnight, the night before Evelyn's funeral.

The morning after he failed to show up at the memorial service, a friend went to Tucker's house on West Dartmouth Street, hoping to find the couple. Nobody answered the door. The friend peeked inside, to see furniture turned over and drawers emptied. The place had been ransacked, but a man's and woman's wallets were there. Empty. Police later found Fred's car, inexplicably

46

Fred Tucker, whose body was found in a Toledo, Ohio, garbage dump, along with the body of his new wife, Louise Caston. (The Herald Palladium, Dec. 22, 1980)

parked in front of a bar three miles south of his home.

The city wondered for three days where they'd gone, until a gruesome discovery in a Toledo, Ohio, landfill hit the newspapers. A guy shooting a bow and arrow at cardboard boxes in a city dump there found the bodies. Toledo, 100 miles south of Flint, was Louise's hometown.

Their bodies were found with wrists and ankles bound. Pillow cases concealed their heads under plastic dry-cleaning bags believed to be taken from Fred's home. Coroners determined they had died from suffocation and police believed they had probably been killed at Tucker's ransacked home, where it appeared the back door had been forced open.

Nobody could figure out the motive for sure, though speculation swirled around Fred's many business dealings and political career. Or could it be a jealous lover, or was he involved with dangerous criminals? Some wondered if it was a professional hit, as his many business and political dealings may have made him some powerful enemies. Others speculated that Fred had walked in on Louise being raped, but semen taken from Louise's body, which might be useful now that DNA forensic science has advanced far enough, has turned up missing from the evidence room, as have a bathrobe and a nightgown.

Police never had enough evidence to lead to any arrests and the grisly deaths of the councilman and his bride remains a mystery four decades later, as the favors and alliances built by a well-liked Flint politician fade into distant memory.

MICHIGAN MUSIC IN A MINOR KEY

Michigan has been a force in music throughout the years. The Motown sound, of course, is the most famous example, making an indelible mark on the soundtrack of America and the world in the 1960s and '70s. It allowed Detroit to join a handful of cities that have their own music style, synonymous with the town, along with Nashville, New Orleans, Memphis and, to a lesser degree, Chicago blues and Philadelphia soul.

It doesn't end there. Such diverse rockers as punk pioneer Iggy Pop, old-time rock-n- roller Bob Seger, rapper Eminem—just to name a few—have also sprung from the Mitten state.

But the local music is not always harmonious. Here are some of the sad or scandalous notes:

WHEN HITSVILLE NEEDED CASH

Berry Gordy brought an organic Detroit sound to the world through Motown Records and its stable of singers, songwriters and studio musicians.

In the early days, he prostituted his wife-to-be Raynoma Liles, and other women, to keep the lights on—and the mics and mixing boards as well—at 2648 West Grand Boulevard, according to Raynoma in her 1990 book, "Berry, Motown and Me." Members of the Gordy family called her accounts false, and Berry Gordy tried to block the book from being sold.

SILENCE AT THE OLDEST JAZZ CLUB

Eddie Jefferson's distinctive jazz-singing voice was silenced on May, 9, 1979, after his last gig at Baker's Keyboard Lounge on Livernois Avenue. As he walked out of the club around 1:30 a.m., someone drove by and shot him. A suspected gunman was identified as a dancer he had fired. Prosecutors didn't have enough evidence to convict him and the accused was acquitted after standing trial.

A SELF-BLOCKED COMEBACK

Del Shannon, born Charles Westover in Grand Rapids, is best known for his 1961 classic hit "Runaway." In the 1980s, he was seeing a bit of a resurgence, recording with Tom Petty, the Smithereens and Jeff Lynne. After Roy Orbison died, Shannon was supposed to join supergroup The Traveling Wilburys with Petty, Lynne, George Harrison and Bob Dylan. But before that ever happened, Del Shannon's chronic depression took over and he committed suicide by shooting himself on February 8, 1990 in Santa Clarita, California.

1972 file photo

Musical icon Marvin Gaye flanked by his parents in happier times. In 1984, Marvin's father, Marvin Sr., shot the singer during an argument. (*The Sacramento Bee*, April 29, 1984)

MARVIN GAYE'S FATHER SHOOTS HIM

Marvin Gaye was a major force in Motown, as a song-writer and singer. In the early '70s, he expanded the soul sound beyond the well-loved, danceable love and loss songs to peace and ecology on his landmark album "What's Going On." He later recorded the ultimate make-out classic, "Let's Get It On."

But the music business took its toll on him, as it did on so many others. While he was staying with his parents in Los Angeles, depressed and with a cocaine habit, he had a bitter argument with his father Marvin Gay Sr. (the singer had changed the spelling of his last name). On April 1, 1984, the elder Marvin shot his son three times in the chest with a gun his famous son had given him as a gift. Marvin Gaye died in his brother's arms, saying he'd wanted to die, but couldn't do it himself. He would have turned 45 the next day.

FEAR IN THE TIME OF CHOLERA

WHERE: YPSILANTI, DETROIT, TRAVERSE CITY, LEELANAU COUNTY, OTHER POINTS IN MICHIGAN
WHEN: 1830s, 1850s, 1910s

IN THE HOT HUMIDITY OF LATE JUNE, WHOSE INESCAPABLE TAUNTING IS LIKE A FLY BUZZING AROUND ONE'S FACE, JOB GORDON, THE TOWN SUPERVISOR OF YPSILANTI, QUILL-SCRATCHED HIS SIGNATURE ON A PROCLAMATION TO KEEP DETROITERS OUT OF THEIR FAIR COMMUNITY.

This wasn't like some late 20th Century "stay-south-of-8-Mile" thing. This was because in 1834, cholera was killing hundreds of people farming in Detroit, or coming and going through the bustling river port town of 5,000 or so.

Ypsilanti hadn't had a problem with it so far, so they attempted to quarantine their town.

Anyone from the D had to have a doctor's note to get into the Y.

Ypsi meant business. Ypsilanti men were known to block the road that led into town. Shots were fired to keep the potential carriers out of town.

Yet unlike the Covid-19 pandemic of 2020, face masks would do no good. It was bacterial, not a virus. You couldn't cough it into someone else's life. You had to poop it, or otherwise introduce it to the unsanitary public water sources. The cholera bacteria would nestle in someone's intestines and then make its way down the chute and into wells and rivers, where everyone got their drinking, cooking and bathing water.

See, wells were shallow and often not far down-stream from outhouses. Single-ply corn cobs and lax hand-washing didn't help much, either.

And 322 Detroiters died of it, including George Bryan Porter, the governor of Michigan Territory. New York, St. Louis and Cincinnati also suffered from what many called The Asiatic Cholera in mustachioed, 1800s parlance. That's because it was first known to appear in the Ganges River delta in India, in about 1817, then found its way over the Himalayas into Russia and was carried by soldiers into Europe.

FARMING IT ... BY WILLARD BOLTE

Cholera was a bacterial illness and was spread around the world in times of relatively primitive sanitation through water and human and animal waste. (The News Palladium, June 30, 1938)

Facing page: Illustration from a flu potion advertisement. (Battle Creek Enquirer, Aug. 14, 1919)

From European ports, merchant sailors then carried it around the globe. The New World got it later than the rest of the planet, but wasn't spared any of the misery. It all took a matter of years—rather than weeks like in the case of Covid-19.

And, as is often the case, the epidemic made life harder for poor people, minorities and recent immigrants—including the vast wave of new arrivals from Ireland. The disease didn't necessarily hit them any harder, but the coincidence of their arrival made people blame them for having brought the disease.

The epidemic gradually subsided, but a second wave of cholera hit the country, and Michigan, in the early 1850s. This time, the toll was about 700 deaths in Detroit, which had grown to 21,000 inhabitants.

Because of better sanitation technology, cholera is now almost non-existent in First World countries. Yet, of course, that's not the end of public health crises.

VICTIM OF FLU
SLEEPS 5 WEEKS

MIRIAM
JOHNSON

The causes and effects of flus and colds were as baffling then as they are now. (Battle Creek Enquirer, March 24, 1919)

The influenza pandemic of 1918 that killed 50 million people worldwide, took the lives of nearly 15,000 Michiganders in the half-year between October 1918 and April 1919. At the start of the outbreak, Gov. Albert Sleeper ordered "places of public amusement" closed, as well as churches. Several schools also closed, though Sleeper left that up to the local districts.

Now, that one was more like the 2020 Coronavirus pandemic in how it was transmitted. Influenza is a virus and could be coughed, sneezed, sung or laughed into everyone else in the room, market, church or whatever.

One thing the viral and bacterial illnesses have in common is quarantining. When Traverse City had a severe outbreak in January 1919, neighboring Leelanau County sought to impose a four-day quarantine on anyone wishing to enter the county. Leelanau leadership asked the state board of health to officially quarantine its borders from possibly disease-carrying Traverse Citians. The board granted the quarantine request and the Michigan State Constabulary sent four officers to guard the main road between the two. (The constabulary came into being in 1917, as home front protection during World War I, and was now transitioning toward what became the Michigan State Police.)

Just like now, doctors advised, begged and pleaded with people into wearing face masks, and they were as controversial then as in the 21st Century. Newspapers carried word of businesses being temporarily closed for not making customers and employees wear masks. A humor piece in the Lansing State Journal asked if men with thick moustaches should be exempt from wearing masks, and the Detroit Free Press had this teaser for the beginning of school in 1918, decrying masks and trivializing female college students: "Unsightly 'Flu' Masks Hide Many a Dainty but Unpowdered Nose as Girls Wend Way to Classes."

Dr. John Harvey Kellogg. (Battle Creek Enquirer, Nov. 29, 1992)

CEREAL BROTHERS SNAP, CRACKLE AND POP

WHERE: BATTLE CREEK
WHEN: LATE 1800s TO MID-1900s

TOGETHER, THE KELLOGG BROTHERS—JOHN THE KOOKY DOCTOR AND WILL THE BUSINESSMAN—CHANGED THE AMERICAN BREAKFAST TABLE AND REVOLUTIONIZED THE FOOD PACKAGING INDUSTRY. BUT MAN, DID THEY HATE EACH OTHER.

From the 1890s to the mid-1900s, Battle Creek was the epicenter of miracle cures and trendy diet fads. When Dr. John Harvey Kellogg became director of a sanitarium founded by the Seventh Day Adventist Church, he put it on the map with his ambition and quirky charisma. He was a prolific author of books touting his medical and health-related theories and edited a magazine on the topic as well. He was in

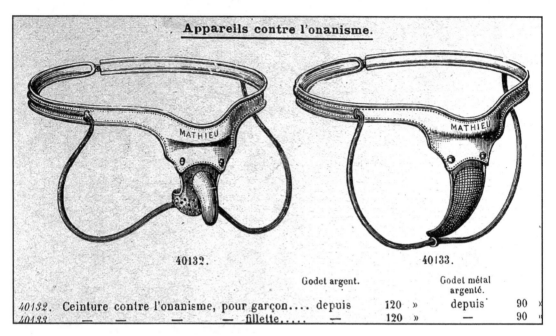

		Godet argent.	Godet métal argenté.
40132.	Ceinture contre l'onanisme, pour garçon.... depuis	120 »	depuis 90 »
40133.	— — — — fillette..... —	120 »	— 90 »

Devices designed to keep men from touching themselves in arousal, which could be caused by overly spicy foods, Dr. John Kellogg taught.

his element as the white-suited celebrity health lecturer with the grandfatherly white hair and Colonel Sanders-esque, Van Dyke beard. He counted among his followers some of the era's elite, including Henry Ford, Thomas Edison, Amelia Earhart and Presidents Taft, Harding and Coolidge.

Kellogg led the nutrition sciences in his crusade to flush out the pioneer diet of cured meats, lard and other stick-to-your-ribs-and-arteries fare. That diet got the hardy souls who had spread out and settled the country through long trails and hard winters, but the grub didn't exactly waltz right through their intestines without raising a little hell along the way. Experts today would agree with Dr. Kellogg's advocacy of fresh air, exercise, laughter and spirituality to improve health, as with his touting the benefits of a plant-based diet.

Yet, while he had some good ideas that were ahead of his time, he also espoused some that seem downright bizarre nowadays. At one point he figured that light therapy (using electric lights to substitute for sunlight) could help with depression. On the other hand, he also thought it could cure syphilis and diabetes. He worked with vibrating chairs, but not the kind that people use now for massages: these were wooden chairs that vibrated like crazy to help shake loose the digestive system. He believed in vigorous exercise and breathing outdoor air, but also designed a slapping machine that was supposed to smack a person's blood circulation into high gear.

Dr. Kellogg was obsessed with bowels and getting them to move, but to sum up two of his other preoccupations: mastication good, masturbation bad. He was a proponent of "Fletcherization," after Horace Fletcher who advocated chewing each bite of food at least 40 times. And, as one of several nods to the Seventh Day Adventists, self-pleasure was an ultimate evil that he said could

cause disease, sap energy and turn the practitioner mopey and grumpy. He taught that people could thwart such "evil desires" by avoiding "exciting and stimulating foods."

He was such an extreme fan of sexual abstinence that he claimed he had never had sex with Ella, his wife of 41 years.

To get boys to stop abusing themselves, Kellogg suggested tying their hands or circumcising them without anesthesia. For girls, he proposed removing the clitoris surgically or with carbolic acid.

A particularly shameful viewpoint he espoused was that of eugenics, a racist and ableist theory that has since been discredited. He and many other successful White people of the late 1800s and early 1900s believed in selective breeding to improve the human race. In other words, they wanted to make hybrid people. Kellogg and many others believed that interracial relations were harmful to the White race, so the philosophy naturally found many enthusiastic disciples among the Nazis.

The Battle Creek Sanitarium before it was destroyed by fire in 1902.

Their father, John Preston Kellogg came to what is now Flint from Massachusetts in the 1830s, during a wave of pre-statehood migration aided by the newly dug Erie Canal. Disease, infant death and general hardship smacked the family hard, as it did many in that time and place.

John and Will were two of the 12 children of John Preston Kellogg who lived beyond infancy. After his first wife, Mary Ann Call Kellogg, died of tuberculosis, he married Ann Janette Stanley, who gave birth to John and Will.

The doctor's brother, Will Keith Kellogg, was eight years his junior, and joined the sanitarium after honing his business acumen selling brooms for his father.

John was the "favorite," Will often said. This might have been partly because John tormented his younger brother and snitched on him for every little transgression, making sure their

parents saw him as a troublemaker. John was bright and studious and his parents and those around them expected him to amount to something big.

Younger brother Will, on the other hand, was quiet and given to melancholy. And, well, Will was doing fine in the broom business. Nobody would have bet that his business chops would someday out-earn and out-influence his brother's sophisticated snake-oil shtick.

To get there, though, he had to do a stint as Doc Kellogg's employee. He sucked up a lifetime of condescension and abuse, meanwhile helping the sanitarium's state-of-the-art kitchen perfect methods for Doctor John's favorite health food invention: grain flakes.

John Kellogg had been experimenting with wheat for some time, and was feeding wheat flakes in milk to many of the sanitarium visitors.

Will, however, thought corn had a richer flavor than wheat. Wheat was fine for Dr. Kellogg, though, as we already discussed the seductive powers of food that tastes good.

Nevertheless, Will continued to explore the flaking characteristics of the Americas' native grain. He kept copious notes on each experimental batch, working to arrive at the best method of rolling the dough, cutting off the flakes and baking them. In addition to its taste, corn had superior texture and the batter was easier to work with. Eventually, Will adopted it as the cereal that would turn the family name into a household word.

Dr. John was mad when he learned that Will's tweaks included adding salt, sugar, malt and other things to make corn flakes taste even better. The doctor's anger heated up more when Will broke off into boxing the corn flakes to sell beyond the sanitarium walls.

Will's endeavor was done partly in desperation, to catch up with rival C.W. Post.

Post was a successful businessman who had come to Battle Creek in the early 1890s to seek help from the famous doc with his ulcers and other stress-related ailments. During his stay among Dr. Kellogg's white-clad disciples, he developed a fondness for the flaked cereals there. He figured the general public would like them too. He brazenly set up shop on the other side of town, first producing the coffee substitute Postum, while working out his own flake-manufacturing methods.

In 1904, Post released Elijah's Manna, a type of corn flake. It didn't take off at first, and some people objected to the name on religious grounds. The company renamed them Post Toasties and sales increased dramatically.

Will was incensed that someone else was capitalizing on their creation, so he started the Battle Creek Toasted Corn Flake Company in 1906. The company would later become Kellogg's. It took off quickly and Americans were snapping up boxes of this new breakfast, which was lighter and easier than anything they were used to.

Dr. Kellogg thought he'd try his hand at mass-marketing cereal, so he sold off some stock from his brother's company and set up to sell his bland flakes under the Kellogg name, too.

That created a problem for Will, now a captain of industry who didn't want people to confuse his brother's flat-tasting flakes with his own popular product. Will sued to keep the doctor's product off the shelves, and John counter-sued for permission to use his name on his own products.

The court fight ate up an entire decade and worked its way up to the Michigan Supreme Court. In 1920, the court ruled unanimously in favor of Will the food-industry pioneer, who had first commercialized corn flakes, over John the health guru who had first turned grains into a bowel-friendly breakfast alternative.

Will now owned the Kellogg name for his products, but it was at the expense of their already fragile relationship. The bitterness remained and the brothers barely spoke to each other for the remaining 23 years of John's life.

John made a kind of truce on his deathbed toward his younger brother in the form of a complimentary letter. The kind words, sadly, didn't reach Will until long after his brother's death. John's secretary had withheld the missive, figuring it was too humble on the part of the great Dr. John Harvey Kellogg.

OCCUPATIONAL HAZARDS IN THE COPPER AND IRON MINES

THE STORY OF THE WESTERN UPPER PENINSULA IS, IN LARGE PART, THE STORY OF MINING. The copper mines centered around the Keweenaw Peninsula and the iron mines stretching from Marquette County to the western end of the U.P. have employed Yoopers on and off for generations.

Starting in the mid-1800s, the mines attracted immigrants from Finland, Italy, Scandinavia, Cornwall and French Canada, producing a colorful mix of languages that melded together into the Yooper accent. The Cornish miners also contributed the quintessential Upper Peninsula food, the pasty—a stuffed dough shell with potatoes, meat, onions and rutabagas—that provided a meal a miner could stuff in his shirt until lunchtime.

But enough romanticizing of a job that required long days in a dank, dark hole and presented many dangers. In the wintertime, miners would rarely see the sun. Chiseling at a tunnel's rock walls caused many a collapse. Add dynamite to the mix and, well, any day on the job could be a death-defying adventure. There were dangers outside the mines, as well. Any efforts to make working the cold tunnels less dangerous often led to violence.

In the early days, the crushed or suffocated bodies of workers were often delivered to a family's doorstep along with a notice from the employer, evicting them from their home, which was property of the mining company.

Fires and floods accounted for two of the state's biggest mining disasters.

On Sept. 7, 1895, a fire started in a copper mine near Calumet, owned by

the Osceola Consolidated Mining Co. The fire fed on a wooden frame built to hold up a particular area of the mine. Some of the workers failed to take it seriously, instead deciding to sit and eat their lunch, figuring it would go out on its own. But it grew and the smoke moved erratically through the connected mines, suffocating the miners who were trying to escape.

The fire ended up killing 30 workers in the mine, some failing to escape even as they clung to a ladder in a desperate effort to get out.

An even worse mining accident occurred in an iron mine near Ishpeming on Nov. 3, 1926. The mine, owned by the Cleveland Cliffs Iron Co. of Ohio, had a maximum depth of 1,060 feet. One worker was using dynamite to loosen ore from the walls of the mine—a common practice, but an obviously perilous one. On that day, the explosion caused a cave-in that sent water gushing down the shaft from a neighboring lake.

Miners sit on cold, sharp rocks with their lunch pails at the Tamarack mineshaft, one of the most productive mines in copper country. Mining was a hard and dangerous job, even more so then than now, and gave a lot to Upper Peninsula culture, including that quintessential bit of Yooper cuisine known as the pasty.

The water trapped many of the 52 miners present, flooding two levels of the mine. Some were able to reach the ladder and attempt to climb out, but the water was coming too fast, and within 15 minutes it had flooded the mine until only 185 feet of the 1,000-foot shaft remained above water.

Wilford Wills recognized the danger early as the whoosh of air following the explosion blew out the carbide lamp on his helmet. He made his way to the ladder and fought against the forceful water spraying into his face. He clung to the rungs for dear life, removing his slippery gloves with his teeth, and arrived at the surface, exhausted, after a desperate climb of 800 feet in 14 minutes. Wills' miracle would not be repeated that day. All 51 of his coworkers died, trapped under the rushing water.

Recovery crews spent the next 17 days searching for bodies, but in the end, they could only bring 10 of them back to the surface. The mine is closed and is now private property with a memorial at the entrance naming all of the victims.

(The Calumet News, Nov. 10, 1913)

MRS. CLEMENC FOUND GUILTY

Case May Be Appealed to the Supreme Court

Mrs. Annie Clemenc, the Calumet woman strike leader, who rejoices in the sobriquet "Big Annie," was convicted in the circuit court this morning of a charge of assault and battery, preferred by Wilfred Kesaniemi.

BIG ANNIE FIGHTS FOR MINERS
• •

The worst disaster in the heyday of Upper Peninsula mines didn't happen in a mine, just as the person most famous for fighting for miners' rights did not work in the mines. But their stories are intertwined.

At six-feet, two-inches tall, most men looked up to talk to "Big Annie" Klobuchar Clemenc. Hair in a bun and wearing a gingham dress, the statuesque Annie was at the front of many protest marches, holding up the American flag on a pole.

Born Annie Klobuchar to Slovenian parents, her father mined copper for Calumet and Hecla Mining Co. As a young teen, she worked at a church helping miners who had been crippled on the job. At 18, she married Joseph Clemenc, pronounced Clements.

Her activism kicked into high gear in February, 1913, when she led the organization of a local women's auxiliary to the Western Federation of Miners in Calumet. On June 23 of that year, the miners went on strike, starting more than a half-year of bitter confrontation and marching against the mining companies. The workers were seeking work days shorter than 12 hours, and better pay, but most importantly they fought for safer conditions. One such hazard they were fighting against was the fact that the dangerous two-man drill was about to be turned into a one-man drill, leaving nobody to seek help if the one man caused a wall to collapse.

Small skirmishes marked the summer months, but escalated in August, when guards shot indiscriminately into a boarding house in the enclave south of Houghton known as Seeberville during a scuffle with disgruntled workers. The bullets hit two immigrant men in the building and killed them.

Annie led that funeral procession.

But the worst of it came in December. Annie and the women's auxiliary hoped to cheer up the children of Calumet who had weathered the strike for six hungry months. They saw their parents scared, angry and out of work, so Annie and the rest of the Women's Auxiliary threw a holiday party on Christmas Eve, upstairs at the Italian Hall. Nearly 700 people showed up for treats, songs and small gifts. A happy child could almost forget the bitterness at home, until, in the middle of the reverie, a mysterious figure in black coat and black beard, yelled "FIRE!"

People rushed for the steep stairway, the only official exit. The crush of people held the door shut and the havoc smothered and trampled many in the crowd. The stampede killed 73 people, mostly children.

Nobody has ever found the person who shouted the false warning, setting the tragedy in motion, though many believe it was someone supporting the mining companies.

And once again, Annie led the massive funeral procession for the shocked, grieving town.

Early in 1914, the strike came to an end, with strikers dispirited and the company making minor concessions. Early that year, Annie toured the Midwest, speaking of the catastrophe and raising money for the families who had lost loved ones. Not long after, she divorced Joseph Clemenc, who turned out to be an abusive alcoholic.

Later, Annie moved to Chicago, where she remarried, had a daughter, and found that her new husband was also a drunk and a wife-beater. She died in 1956 of cancer at age 68.

SO MANY WAYS TO DIE IN THE WOODS

THE RUSH THAT BROUGHT DOWN MOST OF MICHIGAN'S WHITE PINES IN THE 1800s LEFT MORE THAN STUMPS. It left prized woodwork in homes all over the continental United States and it left some rich folklore. It also left eroded hillsides and scraped-out riverbeds.

It's harder to see the human toll. Sure, you can pay a solemn visit to Seney's Boot Hill Cemetery, a final resting place for dozens of anonymous shanty boys—a term for the lumber camp workers before someone coined "lumberjack" in the 1870s. Graves are marked by dents in the ground where the lumberers decayed without a vault to keep the earth from caving in on them.

Chances are, many of the hastily interred met their ends when they failed to hear shouts of "Timber!" and huge limbs or trunks fell on them. Still others tumbled off stacks of logs that started rolling away under their feet. Another possibility was slipping under the tumble of logs down a "rollway"—a steep river-bank over which logs were rolled into the river below—as was falling off a log in a river and having one's head crushed between two floating trunks.

There's no way of knowing how many of the burly or wiry strong men saw their lights go out from a single slip-up. Yet those who cut down the behemoths that measured four times their width and 25 times their height faced many perils in all aspects of their work. Those in the sawmills who cut them into boards have always worked closer to tragedy than most of us. Even now, the industry sits atop the list of perilous professions. The U.S. Bureau of Labor Statistics reported 64 on-the-job deaths per 100,000 workers in 2018 for logging, a rate 16 times that of all other industries combined.

Looking back on the actual dangers themselves provides a fascinating gander at the people who transformed the state into what it is now. It also shines a light on what pampered lives we lead as 21st-Century gadget gazers.

A log slide, somewhere in Michigan, helped lumbermen get logs from the tops of hills to the river. Some slides, often made of wood, let the logs build up enough speed that they would shoot out the end. A person standing in front of where it shoots out didn't stand a chance against the huge wooden projectile.

A historic loggers raft on display along the Highbanks Trail in Michigan's Huron National Forest.

CRUSHED—One particularly gruesome accident led to the naming of a forested hillside overlooking the Jordan River near Alba as Deadman's Hill. (There's another hill south of Lansing that had the name Dead Man's Hill, two words instead of one, until recently. But it was named for an act of violence rather than an accident [see page 131].)

The Alba-area Deadman's Hill got its name from a 1910 tragedy. Stanley "Big Sam" Graczyk was hauling logs down the hill to the river in late May. It was a time of year when three-petaled white trilliums blanketed the forest floors, if they weren't trampled over by the crews. Sam may have anticipated his upcoming wedding as he helped get logs to the river that day. Several others worked the woods around him, mostly chaining logs to the wheels —the horse-drawn log-hauling carts consisting of two wheels about a dozen feet high, between which the logs dangled by chains.

Big Sam was running alongside just such a rig, next to the eveners behind the horses and in front of the logs, when he stumbled and fell. He thought quickly enough to roll out of the wheel's path but his foot caught on the dangling logs. His leg twisted around and pulled him under the wheel, which rolled over him with the full tonnage of the lumber chained to it. Tony Wojchiechowski was waiting on the side of the trail with another log-loaded set of wheels, and he gasped as he watched the huge wheel crush the life out of Sam. Tony rushed over and held up Sam's head. "Are you hurt?" he asked and watched Sam's eyes roll around. The wheel ended the Polish immigrant's 23-year run on the planet then and there.

Down the rollway and into the river. Logs piled up in the spring waiting to be floated down to sawmill towns. The "river hogs" who drove the logs down the rivers, had a particularly skilled and perilous job. Falling under or between the logs could bring a quick end to a lumber worker's life.

Most victims and their deaths soon faded into anonymity, and some camps saw several fatal incidents in a season with barely enough time to bury them—let alone notify the next of kin.

SAWMILLS—The dangers didn't end at the edge of the woods, or after the logs floated down the river. Sawmills were loud, busy places, filled with peril. Josh Wilson was killed at a Mitchell Bros. mill in Jennings when he fell 20 feet off of a chain that carried logs up to the mill.

In Cadillac, on Sept. 28, 1915, Gust Peterson, a 20-year-old man from Leroy, fell on a large, whirring circular saw blade, which sliced Peterson in two, baring bones and spilling his intestines

and other organs. Oscar Backstrom, working near him, fainted at the gruesome sight, a blurb in the Detroit Free Press reported.

DYNAMITE—Near Crystal Falls in April, 1887, late spring ice covered the rivers, preventing the lumber camps from getting their logs afloat. The bosses were itching to get them to the sawmills, while the shanty boys longed to get out of the woods and finally get paid for the work they'd done all winter. In their haste to solve the problem, they figured dynamite would do the trick. Workers placed sticks of it in strategic places to blast the river open. When the fuses reached the TNT, the explosion blew

fire, ice, rocks and wooden shrapnel in all directions. It all rained down on workers as they ran away from it, and several lost their lives that day.

LOG SLIDE—The log slide is like a cross between a Cedar Point ride and a safety inspector's worst nightmare. The slide was a wooden chute or sluice used to send logs from high on a steep hill down to water-level. Thing is, some of those logs picked up a lot of speed coming down that contraption, and on more than one occasion, they shot out of there and took some poor, unsuspecting logger to his final reward.

LOG DRIVES—River pigs, or river hogs, were the guys who rode the logs down the river to the sawmills. French-Canadians and Native Americans were reputed to be the best at the job, so they were often assigned the task. Drownings were common, and in one drive in 1871 on the Chippewa River in Wisconsin, 10 men died in nine days. The Manistee Times reported at least eight deaths in area lumber camps in 1868–69, and that was in early February, when there was still plenty of the season left.

On the drive down the river, the behemoth logs floated downstream with such force that the crashing sound of a sudden log jam could awaken an entire town. When the jams stopped up the river traffic, the river hogs took their peaveys—long poles with a poker and hook on the end—and looked for the keystone logs that could send the whole show moving again with a nudge or a heave. If the bottleneck was at a drop in the stream, the one who got it moving could easily fall and be mangled by the weight of the logs. In fact, "getting sluiced" meant not getting off in time before the logs went down a sluice or a dam. Some ended up buried on the river bank with their boots hung on a tree limb to mark the grave.

DASH FOR CHOW COSTS RIVER HOG HIS LIFE

On the U.P.'s Fence River, a man named Bell was floating logs when it was time for grub. Now, river hogs had to eat quickly while the logs were in motion, so the cooks made the meals in a wanigan, a floating cook shanty. On this particular day, when the dinner bell sounded, Bell was about a mile away from the wanigan. He hopped from log to log, choosing the faster moving ones, in order to get to the cook and avoid missing a well-earned meal. He thought he could make it until the log he was on slammed into a rock and pitched him into the air. He came down, then slipped through a gap and under the logs. That was a deadly place to be. Breaks in the logs might allow his head to rise for a breath of air, but a huge chunk of wood could easily crash into him and crush his head if he did.

Bell was trapped under the logs and died with an empty stomach.

LUMBER BARONS

DURING THE HALF-CENTURY FROM 1860 TO 1910, MICHIGAN WAS THE EPICENTER OF THE LUMBERING INDUSTRY IN THE UNITED STATES. By that time, the old-growth pines in Maine were pretty much depleted, and lumber speculators were eager to continue their march through the continent, from Atlantic to Pacific.

Western expansion was in high gear and the railroad was creating new towns at stops all over the country. That fueled the rush to turn Michigan's vast forests into lumber to build the growing country. The majestic white pines, centuries old and some reaching the height of a 10-story building, brought speculators from all over, though particularly from the eastern U.S. Such grand trees once shaded almost the entire state, though they now only survive at Hartwick Pines, a 49-acre park that Karen Hartwick, born Karen Michelson to a sawmill-owning family, had the foresight to preserve in the 1930s.

Many companies, large and small, competed to chop and saw down the trees, float the logs down the rivers to sawmill towns, cut them into boards and ship them around the country.

Among them were a few big enough for the term "lumber baron" to apply. Here are a couple of the more significant and eccentric among them:

Wellington R. Burt (1831-1919)

LAST WILL AND RESENTMENT

WELLINGTON R. BURT was one of the most successful lumber barons in Michigan, amassing a fortune of up to $90 million ($1.3 billion, today). In the early 1900s, he was among the top ten richest people in the United States.

Burt grew up farming in Jackson County. At age 26, he returned to Michigan from working on merchant ships in the Pacific, from Australia to South America, to work at the Pine River lumber camp in St. Louis. Almost immediately, he was named a foreman and began saving his money to invest in his own lumber businesses. In 1858, after a year of saving his foreman's wages, about $26 a month, he bought 300 acres of wooded land in Gratiot County and started his own company.

His mill became one of the largest in the world, but it burned to the ground within nine years. That didn't ruin him, though,

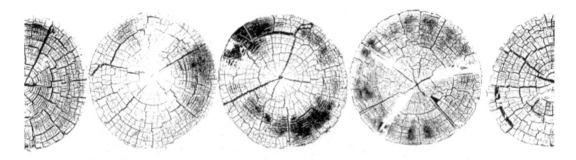

as he'd diversified his holdings by purchasing Minnesota forest land. That land also happened to be in the Mesabi iron range, which allowed him to get his hands into mining, as well. He'd also invested in railroads that served Ann Arbor, Bay City and other points in Michigan.

One story about Burt shows an unfathomable cruelty to animals. He thought his workhorses were getting fat, so he ordered them starved and worked to death. When one man refused to mistreat the animals, Burt supposedly fired him and found someone else to follow his orders.

While Burt built a hospital, schools, an auditorium and other community assets for Saginaw, he's just as well-known now for becoming an ornery, vindictive old cuss who lived out his waning years alone in a mansion with only his servants for company. He had alienated his family and friends and earned the nickname the "Lone Pine of Michigan."

And then he used his will to thrust his middle finger at his family by adding a "spite clause." It stipulated that none of his kin would receive any inheritance (other than the $1,000 to $5,000 crumbs he threw at some of them) until 21 years after the last of his children and grandchildren were dead. His last grandchild kicked the bucket in 1989, and so, in 2011, the fortune was divvied up among descendants who'd never met the successful old coot.

Burt also snubbed the community in that same will. He had planned to bequeath some of his fortune to the people of Saginaw, but after the city increased the assessment on his palatial home, thus raising his taxes, he edited that gift out of the document. He bitterly told the city they were "killing the goose that laid the golden egg."

P.O.'D AND PEED ON

CURTIS EMERSON started a lumber camp near Caro, said to be the first camp in the Saginaw Valley area. He also started the first ferry service in the region and invested in copper and iron mines in the U.P.

He may be best known, however, for a colorful story that paints him as an ornery drunk.

According to the tale, Emerson had started his career in the lumber camps, and even when his growing wealth put him in the company of more refined folk, he never managed to shake off his gruff and crude character. He was said to have had a disagreeable mutt named Caesar, that always padded along by his side. Emerson was easily offended, and when someone crossed him, he'd order his dog, "Piss on him, Caesar. Piss all over him." Caesar was trained to do just that.

LOBBY — BANCROFT HOUSE — SAGINAW, MICH.

The Bancroft House Hotel building, where Curtis Emerson is said to have reduced the fine dinner place-settings to shards, is a red-brick building that is now the Bancroft Apartments, just east of the Saginaw River at the corner of East Genesee and South Washington avenues.

On Sept. 7, 1859, when Saginaw's elegant, four-story Bancroft House Hotel was completed, the proprietors left Emerson off the guest list for the grand opening soiree, though the list included many other lumber magnates.

It stuck in his craw to be left out, but he decided to show up anyway. Uninvited and drunk, he barged into the exclusive affair. Straightaway, he hopped onto the head table that was bedecked with fine crystal and china and a sumptuous feast prepared by the Bancroft's French chef. Emerson stomped down the long table and kicked away at all the settings, sending food and shards of the plates and glasses flying everywhere.

"Send me the bill," he told the owners, before he strutted out of the hotel. The next day, he gladly paid $2,000 to cover the damages, apparently feeling it was all well worth it.

Unfortunately, for those of us who love good stories about irascible characters, the Saginaw County Hall of Fame says the account of the Bancroft episode is bunk. What's more, they say he hadn't really started as a lumberjack, but that he was a well-educated Eastern dandy, and a reasonable and personable chap who actually received an invitation to the Bancroft opening.

However, they do say he liked his drink and enjoyed hosting raucous parties. All of that's relatively easy to let slide, compared to the fact that he was also a Confederate sympathizer during the Civil War.

Those are the two sides of the Emerson legend, and until someone uncovers definitive proof either way, we're all free to accept the entertaining and surly version of Curtis Emerson, or to treat it the way his legendary mutt Caesar might have.

BAY CITY TYCOON MEETS MYSTERIOUS END OR EVEN IN THE NICEST NEIGHBORHOODS

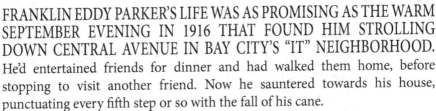

WHERE: BAY CITY
WHEN: 1916

FRANKLIN EDDY PARKER'S LIFE WAS AS PROMISING AS THE WARM SEPTEMBER EVENING IN 1916 THAT FOUND HIM STROLLING DOWN CENTRAL AVENUE IN BAY CITY'S "IT" NEIGHBORHOOD. He'd entertained friends for dinner and had walked them home, before stopping to visit another friend. Now he sauntered towards his house, punctuating every fifth step or so with the fall of his cane.

The cane was all for swagger. He was 49, so his Harvard education was a distant memory, but he was in his prime in the business world. He wore his title—president of the family's lumbering concern Mershon, Eddy, Parker & Co.—like a well-tailored suit.

Parker's evening walk took him past the trolley tracks and the broad-shouldered homes of other well-heeled Bay Citians. A guy like Parker could expect a peaceful amble in such fine environs. He glanced at a passing car, chugging along, as two men crossed the road, heading his way. After the car passed, the strangers ordered Parker to stick up his hands. Parker figured they'd want his gold watch and any cash he was carrying, as he'd never think to carry a bunch of his wealth just walking around the residential streets like this. But before he could even raise his arms, one of the men, fidgeting and darting his eyes back and forth, fired two shots from a .32-caliber pistol, and hit Parker in the arm and back. Parker wheeled around and swung his cane at them.

The men ran away, turning north on Lincoln Street and leaving Parker to walk in circles, dazed. He eventually wandered into the street to try to flag down a car. One vehicle, then another, passed him by, before auto salesman William Bouchey recognized Parker and put on the brakes.

"What's the matter, Mr. Parker?" he asked.

"I've been shot," Parker said, and Bouchey helped him into the car.

Bouchey drove him to the Parker mansion and helped him inside. As Parker's family helped him lead the wounded man in, someone picked

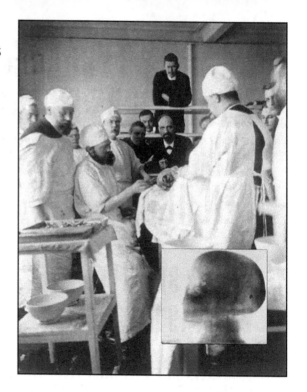

In the operating room of old, surgeons remove a bullet in 1897 after the new technology of X-rays helped them find it. While Franklin Eddy Parker's bullet wound occurred about 20 years later, the scene during surgery may have looked similar. (Photo by Henry Johansson)

up the mouthpiece on the phone and tapped the lever to get an operator to tell them they needed police and a doctor.

Physicians came to his home and tended the wounds. They weren't able to remove the bullets, so they called an ambulance to take him to Mercy Hospital. X-rays showed that the bullet that pierced his back had made its way to his liver. He died on the operating table at 6 a.m.

The news rocked the town, particularly other wealthy neighbors in the Central Avenue district.

Police made it a top priority to solve the murder. They rounded up more than a dozen suspects for questioning. One by one, police interrogated them. One by one, they gave good alibis, or credibly said they knew nothing. One by one, the cops let them go.

Rewards offering up to $3,000 (around $70,000 today) floated around town, but none of them brought in any clues. Police still didn't even have a motive. They never found out why the two young men were there with a gun. Were they going to ask for money, or did someone want popular and powerful Mr. Parker dead?

Meanwhile, the same evening, a peculiar break-in 12 blocks away had detectives naturally looking for a connection. The intruders drew a menacing skull and crossbones, next to a hand, on a table cloth. Whoever the burglars were, the homeowner could only find $10 in cash missing, other than the beer and whiskey to which the burglars had helped themselves.

Two odd crimes in one night. Did they have something to do with each other, police wondered? The only strands running from one to the other were location, and they both seemed to have been the work of young, relatively inexperienced thugs.

That's about as far as it went. After weeks of searching, police ran out of clues, so it went nowhere for about four years.

The case was as cold as Lake Huron on Jan. 15, 1921, when Aloysius "Long Legs" Nowak gave police the best info yet. Police brought him in as a suspect in a southside bank robbery. Perhaps in a bargain for a lighter charge, Long Legs ratted out Stephen Madaj as the gunman who'd murdered Franklin Eddy Parker.

When confronted, Madaj said he had only claimed to be the killer in order to pump up his image among fellow outlaws. But, pshaw, he said he wasn't the real trigger man.

Still, the claim put investigators onto Madaj's scent. With new sources of information, they found Madaj's accomplice from that night four years earlier, Stanley Delestowicz.

In a packed courtroom trial in March, Delestowicz testified that it was Madaj's idea to find someone on Central Avenue to rob. When they told Parker to stick 'em up and he turned around, Madaj overreacted and shot him twice. Then, when Parker remained standing, they freaked out and ran off.

RAMON OLEJNICZAK

While the heat was on, Madaj enlisted to fight for the United States in World War I. When he got back, he worked his way up to leading the South End Gang. They gained a reputation for burglaries, muggings and shootings.

Madaj's lawyer argued that he couldn't be Parker's killer, because he was in Ohio in September 1916, when the murder occurred.

The jury wasn't buying it, and spent a mere 90 minutes convicting him. Then, the judge sentenced him to two life terms, one for an unrelated attempted prison escape.

After four years, Parker's killer was brought to justice, and Madaj saw his criminal career end at age 26.

ALOYSIUS NOWAK

SLUT-SHAMING A DEAD WOMAN

WHERE: BAY CITY
WHEN: 1902

WHEN MAY MORRIS CHECKED INTO BAY CITY'S FRASER HOUSE HOTEL IN FEBRUARY OF 1902, THE DESK CLERK NOTICED HER STRIKING BROWN HAIR AND EYES. JUST SHY OF 30 YEARS OLD, SHE CUT A STYLISH FIGURE, WHICH, IN THAT ERA, MEANT SHE WAS COVERED FROM ANKLE TO CHIN IN A CINCHED-IN DRESS. The 20th Century really hadn't become the 20th Century yet.

In 1902, the Fraser was the nicest hotel in town, and was often busy, so May Morris could come and go with little attention paid. Besides, checking into a hotel in another city for a mysterious operation was common enough in those days for single women who found themselves in an embarrassing situation.

The Fraser House was a four-story, Civil War-era brick building that took up a block near Bay City's often rough and bloody riverfront. It saw its share of well-heeled clientele, riding the trains into town on business, and maybe checking out the hat shop on the ground floor, next to a furnisher.

The staff saw a bit of May Morris over the next month or so. She arrived at the Fraser on Feb. 19 and then checked in again on March 19, staying a few days each time. She whiled away many hours alone in the homey room, and confided in some staffers. She told maids or desk clerks that she lived in Grand Rapids and had come there to have "ear surgery" in her hotel room. She was nervous because she thought she might have to be chloroformed for the operation. Although she claimed to be a stranger in town, she did receive some visitors. First Dr. Roy Griswold toted his bag to the hotel on several occasions, to tend to the woman. Later, Nurse Loretta McEwen started coming.

Oh, and that guy who comes to see her nearly every day, the one with the bushy mustache, the glass eye and the prosthetic arm, that's her uncle, she told the staff.

"Uncle" Edwin T. Bennett, owned the Bay City Tribune and the Lumberman's Gazette, and served as Michigan grand chancellor of the Knights of Pythias, a secret society of dudes. Now 49, Bennett had borne the evidence of a childhood accident since age 11. He grew up near the St. Lawrence River in upstate New York, and tripped on a Civil War landmine while playing on the riverbank one day. The blast robbed him of an arm and an eye, but he rose above the disadvantage quite well.

And now, his um, niece, yeah niece, was expected to undergo the "ear surgery" on March 23. After the operation, Nurse McEwen started checking up on her, staying with Miss Morris as she was tossing and turning, grabbing her gut and doubling over in pain. She had an infection known as Peritonitis, an inflammation of the abdominal lining that protects several organs. Her condition worsened day by day. The nurse may have rolled her eyes, or may have even felt insulted, when Dr. Griswold reminded her to check the ailing woman's ears, as if she couldn't see that it was her gut, not her ears. Nurse Loretta knew the young woman had undergone a tragically botched abortion. One evening, paying a call on the patient, Dr. Griswold pulled the nurse aside, and said, "She won't make it." Nurse Loretta stayed at her side, watching the clock tick past midnight and toward 2 a.m., as the mysterious young woman's breathing slowed down to nothing.

Loretta noted the time of death, gathered her things and took the elevator to the lobby. She stopped at the front desk and told the night clerk to summon a doctor to declare May Morris dead.

Police Chief Nathaniel Murphy got word from the doctor and came in to ask a few questions. Of course, he didn't buy that someone would come from Grand Rapids, across the state by train or carriage, to get an ear operation in a hotel room. He talked to the nurse, and then to Bennett, then Griswold.

NATIONAL POLICE GAZETTE.

NEW-YORK, SATURDAY, MARCH 13, 1847.

THE FEMALE ABORTIONIST.

The cover of the National Police Gazette, March 13, 1847.

He asked Bennett why he visited the attractive young woman every day. He asked why Bennett would pay for her room and her, ahem, ear operation. The nervous publisher had no good answers, and it was obvious to Chief Murphy that Bennett had been having an affair with her.

While Murphy conducted interviews, his officers were trying to find the dead woman's next of kin, but couldn't locate any records of a May Morris in Grand Rapids.

That's because the young woman's real name was Agnes Eberstein and she came from Battle Creek. Her family was still there, so now came the sad task of loading Agnes' body on a train headed home. The prosecutor also sent a doctor onboard the train to watch the undertaker perform his grim duties, so that the doctor could have a closer look at any further clues the body might yield.

As police in Bay City talked to Bennett, he figured his best defense was a mean offense. "She's been on the turf for some

73

Agnes Eberstein (left) the tragically-fated woman known in Bay City at first as May Morris, and Edwin T. Bennett (right), the wealthy newspaper owner who had her undergo a shoddy abortion to cover their affair. (Detroit Free Press, June 13, 1902)

time," he said. He said that the woman's "respectable" parents had told her to "lead a better life," or don't bother to come home. When police asked Bennett about him paying for her room, he said a friend of the Eberstein family had given him the money to pay for it, and to take care of the poor, misguided woman. He said the family wanted her lascivious behavior kept a secret.

Griswold joined in on the cacophony of slurs, adding that Agnes Eberstein had undergone seven abortions, and came to him after the one in Detroit caused her serious health problems. "It was no business of mine to denounce her," Griswold said, denouncingly.

Police Chief Nathaniel Murphy wasn't having it, these defendants trashing this woman, a victim, who had obviously undergone an illegal operation that ended up killing her. One of these guys paid for that criminal medical procedure, and the other performed it, he believed.

Police arrested both men on charges of manslaughter. They both bonded out easily, and pleaded not guilty. They spoke with their lawyers and awaited a trial that would turn into the word of two influential men against a woman who was gone and couldn't defend herself.

Of course, the prosecutor went first. He said Bennett paid for Eberstein's abortion and Dr. Griswold performed it. The illegal procedure, done poorly, led to Eberstein's deadly infection.

The defense resorted to what we would now call "slut-shaming." Bennett and Griswold talked down the dead woman as loose, possibly a prostitute. She'd made a spectacle of herself trying to seduce Bennett at a Knights of Pythias meeting, witnesses said.

The jury wasn't convinced, however, and after 90 minutes of deliberation, found Bennett guilty of manslaughter.

Judge Theodore Shepard sentenced him to seven years in Jackson State Prison. "Inside of one year, from the time she met you, she was in her coffin, and you before the court," Shepard said, scolding Bennet.

He served two of those seven years, before Gov. Aaron T. Bliss commuted his sentence.

Griswold faced trial after Bennett and his defense included evidence suggesting that he had not performed the abortion, and that Agnes had gotten it in Detroit. However, Griswold had helped coordinate and cover up the operation, the jury decided. The judge sentenced the doctor to two years at Ionia Reformatory, but he also received a pardon from the governor and served less than a year.

A STREETCAR NAMED DESTROY

WHERE: MUSKEGON
WHEN: 1919

IN 2020, WE DON'T THINK TWICE ABOUT A PENNY. WILL WE PICK ONE UP OFF THE GROUND? MEH, DEPENDS.

Yet on August 5, 1919, a one-cent raise for a streetcar ride in Muskegon infuriated riders so much that they started pushing rail cars off their tracks in a huge protest-by-vandalism spree.

Muskegon had lost its place as one of the big lumber towns in the state, and lumber magnate Charles Hackley and other business leaders had talked new industries into moving into town. The city grew by 50 percent in the 1910s, and now 36,000 people called it home. Most of them still depended on the trains and trolleys for transportation to and from their low-paying jobs (though the next decade would see people buying cars in record numbers, and helping to turn automobiles from a luxury to a necessity).

The Muskegon Traction & Lighting Co. raised its streetcar fares from 6 cents to 7 cents for a one-way ride to work on Aug. 5, 1919. That was no small change to the people who rode the cars to the factories and docks where they took in maybe $14 a week. That had to pay for the commute, as well as food and rent, and even now, would only be about $215 a week.

The one-cent price hike was the last straw. Their resentment rose to well above a simmer. This was August, in the heat of the summer, and anger often rides the heatwave. All it took was that crucial extra penny to make the steam blow the lid right off.

Tensions began to mount with a group of people venting and arguing with a streetcar conductor. Others started to gather around the trolley tracks. Their numbers grew and soon swelled to several hundred dissatisfied citizens milling about, feeding on the complaints, shouts and anger of those around them.

As tempers rose, someone smashed in a trolley window. It turns out others liked that idea, and it became a flash trend. Police fired warning shots, but the crowd just got louder and more fired up. Push came to shove came to heave-ho, and groups of protesters threw their weight into sending cars downhill. The passenger

75

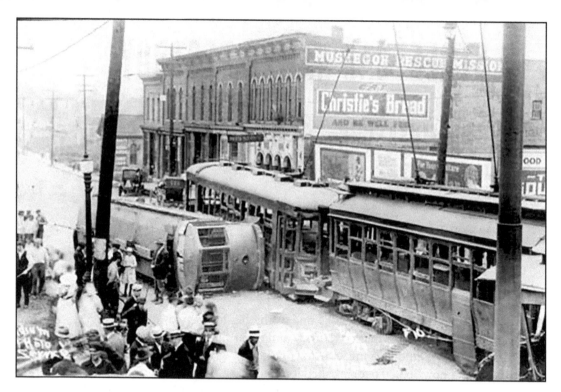

Commuters heavily damaged and tipped over rail cars in a vandalism spree to protest increased train fares.

cars coasted down and crashed into one another, knocking over a couple of the trolleys here and there.

By the time the mob panted for breath and the sweat cooled on their shirts, 13 cars lay dented, broken and at violent angles where Pine and Jefferson streets meet. Some police were said to have run for cover from the mob.

The damage came to $125,000 or so, the equivalent of $1.5 million now.

It just so happened that the city aldermen were having a meeting when the riot was raging, in sight of the city hall. When Gov. Albert Sleeper heard that, he was incensed with the local government. He sent a letter slamming the aldermen and the police for standing by "during the progress of the tumult." He asked why nobody approached the crowd with a bullhorn to see if they had a legitimate beef.

As for the streetcars, they never recovered, and are now on the scrap-heap of history with much of mass transit in the United States.

During WWII, tanks move along a Chrysler assembly line in Detroit.
(Library of Congress)

WAR-TIME RIOT

WHERE: DETROIT
WHEN: 1943

WHILE U.S. ARMED FORCES FOUGHT WORLD WAR II ON THREE
CONTINENTS AND AT SEA, THOSE LEFT ON THE HOMEFRONT
WORKED TOGETHER IN A SPIRIT OF COOPERATION AND
HARMONY TO PROVIDE THE WEAPONS AND MATERIALS THE
MILITARY NEEDED TO DEFEAT THE AXIS POWERS. RIGHT?

Not exactly.

Detroit was nicknamed the Arsenal of Democracy as its numerous
automotive plants retooled to build bomber planes, jeeps, tanks and engines
to wage the conflict. That meant thousands of new jobs for men and women
to work in the factories and foundries, which bulged and strained the city's
housing and services to levels never seen before or since. In a few short

Three African-American workers complete the pilot's compartment of an aircraft in 1942. The promotion of three Black workers on the production line of the Packard Motor Co. plant in Detroit in 1943 led to a walkout, when White workers learned they would have to work alongside them. The plant made plane engines for the U.S. military during World War II. (U.S. National Archives and Records Administration)

years, 350,000 people moved to town, particularly from Southern states, to earn a middle-class wage and to do their part for the war effort. About 50,000 of them were black, as the factories hired across racial lines out of necessity as much as enlightenment.

Living and working side-by-side with people of another race didn't sit well with many of those workers. Competition for housing added to the strain, and by June 1943, feelings of tribalism had built up to the breaking point.

On the third day of the month, a Thursday, about 1:30 in the morning, White workers on the graveyard shift at the Packard Motor Co. plant learned that their bosses had just promoted three Black workers to the final production line. That meant the White employees would have to start working alongside people of a different color—and they weren't about to let that happen.

That morning, 25,000 White employees walked off the factory floor in protest. These sentiments played out elsewhere, as well. Workers walked out of plants in Los Angeles; Beaumont, Texas; and Mobile, Alabama; among other places.

Throughout the next day, protesting workers milled about the gates and

(Detroit Free Press, June 4, 1943)

Workers at Detroit's Packard Plant ignored the union representatives urging them to get back to work.

pressured workers, walking in for other shifts, to join their strike. This brought the plant's output of naval and attack-plane engines to a near standstill. United Auto Workers leaders drove around the entrances in sound trucks and blasted messages to the strikers urging them to go back inside, work together and show solidarity with their fellow employees. Working was the patriotic thing to do, the union argued, and it would show support for the soldiers relying on those engines. The UAW also asked the members to trust them to work it all out in a meeting scheduled for that Sunday.

But there would be no choruses of 'Kumbaya' here. Strikers booed and jeered the speeches. They also ignored the National War Labor Board when its members urged them back to work.

Some of the White workers tried to sound woke, or at least a 1940s version of it, by saying they didn't begrudge the Black workers their promotions. Well, that is, as long as they didn't have to work next to them.

The company, union and government quickly investigated how it all started, named a group of workers as the instigators and then suspended them. They blamed the strike on the Ku Klux Klan.

Apparently, economic concerns won out and, at the beginning of the Sunday night shift, 80 percent of the workers carried their lunch boxes through the gates and the strike was declared over. The three Black men kept their promotions.

The governor banned beer during the riot. Here, thirsty Detroiters eagerly belly up to the bar after the ban is lifted. (Detroit Free Press, June 25, 1943)

But raw feelings still festered throughout the city for the next couple of weeks.

Racial tensions erupted once more on Sunday, June 20, on Belle Isle, the popular island park in the Detroit River. Clashes between Black and White groups escalated throughout the day. What started with words ended with fists and knives. Just like in the strike, the actual rioting broke out in the middle of the night, this time as people were crossing the bridge from the island. The violence spread across the Belle Isle Bridge and to Gabriel Richard Park on the mainland side. The melee had broken out just before midnight, too late for any more than a middle-of-page-one brief in the next day's Free Press, informing readers that the police department had sent 50 officers to try to tamp down the unrest. But the anger burned too hot for police

to put out, and the chaos continued into the next day and beyond.

White groups roamed up and down Woodward Avenue, attacking any Black man they saw. A gang of Whites knocked a trolley off its wire to stop it, then ran aboard to pound the two men of color riding it. The gang beat the victims nearly unconscious before police arrived. Mobs pushed over cars driven by Black people, opened the gas-tank covers and tossed matches into the gasoline pouring out onto the street. When police arrested a White teen for throwing rocks, a mob surrounded the patrol car demanding they "Let him go!" Overwhelmed, the cops let him go.

In predominantly Black areas, African Americans also attacked and beat Whites and looted White-owned businesses. Police patrolled the edges of minority neighborhoods and intercepted Whites trying to enter them, telling them to turn around and stay out of trouble.

Despite a strong police presence, including officers pushing crowds back with tear gas or wielding nightsticks from horseback, law-enforcement failed to restore peace to the streets of the Motor City. People on the street told stories of atrocities—some true, some embellished, others just plain false—that added to the anger. Officers spent much of their time getting the injured to Detroit Receiving Hospital, where orderlies wheeled extra beds into conference rooms to accommodate them.

At one point, police were told a group of Black men was marching toward a precinct, so they geared up to meet force with force. It turned out, however, that the group was a team of air-raid wardens—who generally told people to turn out lights during air-raid drills—intending to walk the streets and keep the peace.

There were cooler heads, but mostly they didn't prevail. Would-be peacemakers appealed to the rioters' sense of humanity, faith and patriotism. The riled mob was having none of their talk of peace, love and understanding. A Catholic priest asked a gang to leave an African American family alone, but a man told him to butt out. "I'm a religious man myself," he told the priest, "but we're up against a situation here that religion can't solve. You've no business here."

At Woodward and Mack, a young man stood on a car bumper and implored the rioters to stop, saying, "This is no way to act while our country is at war." Revelers told him to shut up and threatened to beat him, too.

A woman with a European accent told people she was upset that this could happen here in a democracy. Another woman told her, "You better not stick up for that race, or you're going to be in trouble yourself."

And they ignored a sailor on leave who told people to let a young African American man alone, saying a Black soldier he knew had saved a couple of lives. "You guys are stirring up something that we're fighting to stop," he said.

After about two days, the riots lost steam on their own. Gov. Harry Kelly, who had declared martial law early in the conflict, lifted it so that baseball and horse racing could resume. Odd priorities in a time of great violence perhaps, but he was concerned with making a statement about the city returning to normalcy.

When the fighting subsided, it left bashed-in business fronts and overturned automobiles. It left families and friends to mourn the 34 people who died in the violence, 25 of them African American and several shot by police.

Mayor Edward Jeffries and other leaders at the time blamed the riots on young, unemployed men of color. Many years later a study of arrest records found that many of the White rioters drove in from outside the city, while the injured and arrested Black people were close to their own homes, suggesting a more defensive role.

But of course, Detroit's racial problems were far from over, as evidenced by phenomena like the destruction of a vast African American neighborhood for a freeway cloverleaf in the early 1960s, the 1967 riot—or uprising, as it's now called—and massive White flight to the suburbs for decades afterward.

SEX SELLS: AN EARLY CAMPAIGN AGAINST HUMAN TRAFFICKING

IN THE 21ST CENTURY, HUMAN TRAFFICKING HAS BECOME A POPULAR CAUSE. But it's been around a long time. The subject came into the American limelight in the 1880s, with prostitution booming in Michigan and Wisconsin.

Newspaper stories told of young women tricked and forced into working at brothels that served lumber camps and mining towns throughout the Northwoods, meaning the woods in these two Midwestern states. Some accuse the accounts of being sensationalized to tug at heartstrings, trigger rage, and ultimately sell papers. On the other hand, women's and religious groups reacted with outrage, believing the problem to be rampant and the worst stories to be the norm. Mayors, community-promoting businessmen and governors often downplayed the reports, or denied the sex industry's existence altogether. Historians now believe the truth to lie somewhere in the middle.

By 1886, the newspaper medium had started to popularize the term "white slavery." The phrase was first used in the 1840s in reference to Christians being forced into slavery on the southern shores of the Mediterranean Sea, or to European concubines in Turkey. But the news accounts were co-opting it for prostitution in general, as they detailed beatings, addictions and disease dealt to the women who worked in "dens of iniquity" in Michigan and in Wisconsin.

Similar stories from London may have sparked U.S. reporters' interest in the world's oldest profession.

The laying of telegraph cables across the Atlantic Ocean floor had assisted in the spread of these sensational stories. It used to take weeks by ship for the lurid tales to arrive on our shores, but they now got here within days of their appearance in Great Britain.

As reporters began writing about the same issues here, they discovered a thriving prostitution industry in the Upper Great Lakes region, with all the men moving there to work in lumber camps or mines.

A 19th Century illustration shows lumberjacks giving women a ride on a log-transport sled. It's not certain how often scenes like this played out, but there were hundreds of men and few women in the vicinity of many of the lumber camps. That made it a growth market for the prostitution industry.

FACING: The procurement of girls to serve as "comfort women" in the Americas was widespread enough to appear in this early 18th Century print by French painter Antoine Watteau.

The brothels were attracting, enticing and tricking hundreds of young women to shake loose some dollar bills from the lonely working stiffs.

Minnie Pine was in her early 20s when she made her way from Elmira, N.Y., to Chicago, and then to a bawdy house in the Upper Peninsula, near Iron Mountain. Her story hit the papers and was widely circulated after she was rescued from the life.

According to the story, as it appeared in the Buffalo Sunday Morning News (N.Y.), Minnie Knapp Pine went to Chicago with her husband. While there, he left her, because her "bad habits" caused his "...life to be made very unhappy. She was over-fond of stimulants and fast young men." (The writer of the story apparently didn't give Minnie a chance to refute his claims.) She soon took a job at a restaurant, where her boss William Gaines offered her better pay to work at a lumberman's hotel. She trekked with him to the "immoral resort" in the U.P. and found a house hidden behind a tall, plank fence. As they went through the gate, baying dogs strained at the ends of chains.

When they got inside, Minnie saw a dozen or more women in tights and short dresses drinking with men. She realized

An alarming newspaper ad claims that white slavery will kill 60,000 young women per year, and will be looking for replacements.

what she was expected to do and said she wanted to leave. Gaines warned her that if she did, the dogs would rip her to pieces. She headed toward the door and two men intercepted her and knocked her down. A "big-booted lumberman" approached her and she refused him, so the owner beat her until she succumbed. Upstairs, two women held her down so the lumberman could rape her.

The pimps beat the women daily to break their spirits. Bartenders served the customers overpriced drinks, and the women drank with the men. They didn't dare refuse to do so, or they would be beaten and fined. Minnie tried to escape three times and was run down by dogs. She tried to send letters to relatives, but they were intercepted and destroyed. Women were often sold from one house to another to offer fresh faces for the customers. Police and sheriff's deputies were regular customers, and when

Minnie pleaded with one of them to help her break out, he told the owners, who beat her black and blue as punishment.

Finally, a local politician, persuaded by public sentiment, looked into the house and talked the sheriff into raiding it. Officers arrested Minnie and eight other women, and two men who were running the house. All of them received sentences of one year in the Detroit House of Correction in Plymouth Township, though Minnie and some of the other women were released for health reasons. According to the news story, Minnie was "very low from her usage and cannot live long."

A friend of Gaines spoke up in his defense, claiming that Minnie Pine went to the brothel of her own free will. He also showed a picture of the women there wearing long, modest dresses, and said the dogs were there to keep curiosity seekers out, not to keep the women in.

Newspapers around the country reprinted the article, only a few paragraphs long, but packed with drama.

A woman named Julia Howden told a similar story about her own captivity at a house in Marinette, Wisconsin, a town on the border of the two states. The houses were often located near the state line so they could cross back and forth between states when the heat was on from one direction or the other.

Stories about sex slavery continued to appear in newspapers and magazines. Readers couldn't get enough of them because, well, sex sells. Some, however, became outraged and sought reforms in

Another illustration claims that ice cream shops and fruit stores are places where many women take "their first step downward" to white slavery. Apparently, the chap in the derby has less than noble intentions.

the law that would protect the women caught up in the business. The Woman's Christian Temperance Union in both Michigan and Wisconsin implored their governors to investigate the matter.

In the summer of 1888, Michigan Gov. Cyrus Luce sent inquiries to community leaders throughout the "northern peninsula." That effort supposedly didn't locate a single den. That was good enough for Gov. Luce. No problem. Let's move on.

Wisconsin Gov. Jeremiah Rusk hired a detective who found some quiet, well-run houses in which women were there because they wanted to be. A pimp told the detective that the women were former street walkers or came from worse houses in Milwaukee and Chicago. In other words, this pimp claimed he was offering them upward mobility. The governor's detective claimed that the women employed at the houses were not innocent girls, but women who had been in the business for some time already.

Dr. Katherine Bushnell of the temperance union in Wisconsin wasn't satisfied, though, so she began her own, more thorough, investigation. She visited the towns and personally interviewed and re-interviewed nearly 600 women working as prostitutes. She concluded that white slavery was pervasive in the northwoods. Brothel keepers were raking in the cash, while the law, the press, politicians and other pillars of the communities either looked the other way or actively helped the pimps and madams. Some business owners figured

the houses of ill repute helped promote and diversify the economies of their fair towns. Physicians, too, frequently made good money examining the women for venereal diseases while ignoring their scrapes and bruises. And police were known to capture and return women running away from the brothels that employed them.

Dr. Bushnell's assertions caused just as much controversy as those glossing over the issue. Some accused her of sensationalizing the findings in order to rouse people into action. A piece in the Milwaukee Daily Journal attacked Bushnell—not for her findings, but for her looks. The piece irrelevantly described her as "not what one would call an artist's dream, unless the artist had lunched on mince-pie and pickles before going to sleep on a rail pile."

While the paper frump-shamed Dr. Bushnell, prostitution laws often

Dr. Katherine Bushnell investigated Northwoods prostitution and determined it was rampant and abusive toward the women it recruited. A journalist refuted her, not on her findings, but on her unglamorous appearance.

encouraged slut-shaming. In Wisconsin, it was only illegal to entice a woman into the sex business if she was previously "chaste."

While it's likely that some women were tricked or coerced into the business, others did choose to ply the trade. Jobs for women were few and poorly paid. Some saw prostitution as a higher-paying option. Yet once employed in the business, they often found that madams and pimps gouged a huge chunk of their earnings by charging exorbitant prices for their rooms, food and clothing.

In addition to Minnie Pine, Michigan has other dark stories of the 19th-century flesh business.

James Carr and Maggie Duncan ran what locals called the Devil's Ranch in Harrison, just one of 21 such establishments in Clare County at the time. Carr is said to have beaten to death one of the young women who worked for him after she refused to dance with a customer. The pair was eventually tried and convicted after a man Carr hired to dispose of a buried body turned on Carr and ratted him out.

Near the short-lived iron-smelting town of Fayette on the Lake Michigan side of the Upper Peninsula was Jim Summers. He is believed to have run an ad in a Milwaukee newspaper looking for a young, single woman to care for his supposedly ailing wife. He was really running a whorehouse and wanted her to service his customers. The woman tried to flee and he beat her savagely. After she made her way back to town, a large group of townsfolk hunted Summers down, beat him and left him for dead.

And the town of Seney, on the Lake Superior side of the U.P., boomed for about 15 years as a lumbering town, and is said to have had at least three brothels during its heyday.

In the end, despite the public interest, little was done about the industry, problem or not. Instead, interest in it subsided as the lumber boom played out and as more women and families moved in and replaced the transient male populations. Prostitution was later viewed as more of an urban phenomenon and as the issue resurfaced in the early 20th Century, and then again in the 21st Century, but the narrative was no longer centered in Michigan and Wisconsin.

MASERATI RICK'S CASKET

WHERE: DETROIT
WHEN: 1988

RICHARD CARTER SR. ACHIEVED POWER AND NOTORIETY IN DETROIT'S UNDERWORLD IN THE 1980s WORLD OF DEALING CRACK COCAINE. HIS CASKET, THOUGH, IS WHAT MADE HIM REALLY INFAMOUS BEYOND THAT WORLD.

Carter's friends and criminal cohorts dubbed him Maserati Rick, honoring a particularly flashy set of wheels he'd owned and in which he would screech up to the clubs in style. Yet he was buried in a Mercedes Benz—a $16,000 ($35,000 today) box made to look—well, sort of—like a luxury sedan with moving wheels, working lights and a grille and hood ornament in the style of the German luxury car. That symbol of excess worried people, thinking it might encourage young men from the inner city who already see selling drugs and other crime as their only way to money and status.

Never mind that he was dead at 29, executed in his hospital bed by a rival. For half of his short life, he'd lived a criminally distorted version of the American Dream.

Maserati Rick started as a daring and able teen in the 1970s, working for a car-theft ring. At a time in life when many kids dreamed of any old set of wheels to use on dates, Carter tooled around Detroit in a BMW. At an age when many kids looked into community college, Carter was convicted of receiving stolen goods.

Five years later, in 1982, he was released. For a while, he focused on managing his brother Greg Carter's career in the boxing ring at the famous Kronk Gym on the city's west side. He also served as a bodyguard for a time for his childhood friend Thomas "Hitman" Hearns. Hearns was a locally grown boxer who became the first ever to earn world titles in five separate weight classes.

But crime had been lucrative for Carter before prison, and when a drug sweep put prominent dealers Sylvester "Seal" Murray and members of Young Boys Inc. behind bars, Carter and his friend Demetrius Holloway stepped up to fill the void. First, they started dealing heroin and became allied with Richard Wershe, known as "White Boy Rick" (see page 90), a 16-year-old dealer who had ties to

(*Detroit Free Press*, Sept. 17, 1988)

Richard Carter never saw the age of 30, as he departed this world in a casket made to look sort of like a Mercedes automobile.

some of the recently incarcerated drug kingpins. For protection, they linked up with Reginald "Rockin' Reggie" Brown's gang of hired guns.

Carter laundered his money through several types of small businesses, including hair salons and barber shops. Car washes also were useful as cover in more ways than one. In addition to hiding the true source of his earnings, he could have his dealers drive into a bay, close the door, and while the steam and suds was getting started, load up the car with drugs or cash. After that, the car drove out clean on the outside and dirty as all get-out on the inside.

By the mid-to-late 1980s, Carter controlled the drug trade on the city's east side and had well-established tentacles in Grand Rapids, Kalamazoo, Lansing, Saginaw and Port Huron. His army of underlings—known as the "Best Friends"—helped him amass a reputed $20 million fortune (worth $45 million today) and left a suspected trail of 100 or so corpses of those who tried to stand in their way.

Carter had no shortage of enemies, though a rivalry with a former ally proved particularly bitter. Edward "Big Ed" Hanserd had cut his teeth selling marijuana supplied by Carter and Holloway, but eventually began using competing drug sources and started cutting into Carter and Holloway's territory. Hanserd may have also owed Carter a substantial sum of money. The conflict progressed f om raunchy insults—Hanserd suggested Carter's mother was the one who named him "Big Ed"—to gunshots here and there. In one attempt on Hanserd's life, Carter shot him in the stomach. Recovering from the serious wound, Hanserd refused to tell police who shot him, both out of a sense of honor among criminals, and a desire to exact revenge in a more personal way.

Hanserd knew he was marked for paybacks, so he cooled his heels for a time in Mississippi, then came back north, where he was suspected of two drive-by shootings. The first one sprayed bullets at the home of Carter's mother while she stood on the front porch holding Maserati Rick's 2-year-old son. The second was intended for the home of the child's mother, but instead pelted the home next door.

Then, on Sept. 10, 1988, Hanserd and a friend drove to one of Carter's car washes and opened fire. This time it was Carter's turn to get shot in the gut by Hanserd, but nobody got away unscathed as Carter managed to hit both his assailants in their arms.

Two days later, with another serious abdominal injury, Maserati Rick lay recuperating in room 307 at Mount Carmel Mercy Hospital, when someone disguised in doctors' scrubs walked in and shot him in the face.

While Richard Carter Sr., dead at 29, was already infamous in the Motor City, the funeral and his glitzy coffin spread his notoriety well beyond Michigan. Six Rolls Royces and twelve limousines lined up outside the Peace Chapel to take his body to its final resting place in Elmwood Cemetery, east of downtown.

Newspapers took flak for publishing pictures of him laid out in gaudy style. He became one of the better-known symbols of the drug-fueled violent era that devastated the poorer sections of urban America in the 1980s. Even his mother, Betty Carter, objected to the flamboyant send-off to her high-flying, young-dying son. But another of Carter's brothers told her, "Rick lived this way. He should die this way."

Two years later, Carter's crime partner Demetrius Holloway was shot to death in a clothing store in downtown Detroit. An associate of Hanserd's, Lodrick "The Hitman" Parker—whose nickname implied a more deadly variety of hits than Carter's old friend Thomas Hearns—was accused of both murders. He faced a trial and was acquitted on all charges.

ONE-WAY FAVOR: THE WHITE BOY RICK STORY

WHERE: DETROIT
WHEN: 1980s–2020

RICHARD WERSHE JR. PUT HIS 14-YEAR-OLD LIFE ON THE LINE BACK IN THE 1980s TO HELP THE FBI AND DETROIT POLICE CATCH COCAINE AND CRACK DEALERS. He's said to be the youngest FBI informant ever, and he became the longest-serving, nonviolent juvenile offender in Michigan history.

Wershe is better known under his nickname, "White Boy Rick," which is also the name of a 2018 movie about his life.

Rick Wershe Jr. was growing up on the east side of the city, close to Grosse Pointe, but on the rougher side of the stark border with Detroit. His best friend was Boo Curry, who lived down the street with his family, including his older brother Johnny Curry, a powerful east-side drug gang leader.

When Wershe was 14, he started to grow up much faster.

For one thing, Richard's father, Rick Sr., was operating outside the law himself. He sold firearms and silencers at gun shows and out of the trunk of his car. Often, the firepower and the accessories were outside of what the law allowed. When Feds and Detroit cops started breathing down his neck in the mid-80s, he kept himself out of jail by agreeing to give them information on the drug dealers in the neighborhood. This was the dawn of crack, an unrefined, cheap and highly addictive form of cocaine that was plaguing Detroit and other cities. Narcotics was a hotter topic than illegal firearms, so the elder Rick Wershe entered into a symbiotic relationship with the FBI and local police.

Rick Wershe Sr. fed the investigators information about the local drug scene for a while, but the cops and agents were getting tired of dealing with him. He was always asking for more money, and his information was sometimes questionable. Once, as the Feds and city cops visited their home on Hampshire Street to ask Rick the dad about some of the gangs dealing drugs in that area, Rick the boy heard their questions from another room and peeked out to comment.

Quickly, the investigators realized that the 14-year-old boy knew more than his father about the neighborhood players. They dropped their questioning of Senior, and turned to Junior for info.

Being an informant wasn't a bad gig for a kid, mortal danger aside. Police provided him with cash to buy drugs as a way to get better information.

(Detroit Free Press, Sept. 18, 1990)

Richard Wershe Jr., "White Boy Rick", who became the longest-serving nonviolent juvenile offender in Michigan.

And they gave him enough extra money to pay him for his troubles. The law enforcers seemed to have no qualms about having an 8th grader put himself in harm's way to help their investigations. Rick was happy with the arrangement, as well, as it put money in his pocket. In fact, he was earning about $30,000 a year (equivalent to more than $70,000 today)—obviously way more than enough to allow a teenager to buy fashionable clothes, pay for dates, and get him an enviable car (even though he couldn't legally drive it yet).

Young Rick spent a lot of time with Boo Curry, so Johnny Curry got to know him. Little by little, Johnny grew to accept Rick and even allowed him to hang out with him and his friends. "I felt like he was cool," John Curry said years later. Tall, straight-haired Wershe stood out among the black gangs, usually being the only White guy in the group, and that's why Johnny Curry dubbed him "White Boy Rick." Curry never suspected Rick was talking to cops, "because he was so young."

But then, police arrested some of Curry's associates, based on Wershe's information. Even then, Curry still didn't suspect Rick of working with the cops, but John "Johnny Slim" Walker, a member of the Curry gang, may have figured it out. In November 1984, Rick was visiting Walker's home when Walker called out to Rick to come upstairs. When Rick got to the top step, Walker shot him in the gut, sending him tumbling down the stairs.

The injury was serious and Rick was in for an extended stay at the hospital. When he was well enough, police questioned him about the shooting. Rick insisted it was an accident. When he healed, he had to use a colostomy bag, but his street cred was intact, since he said it was an accident and declined to seek charges against Walker.

Five months later, he was in the Curry gang's graces enough to accompany them to Las Vegas to see Detroit's favorite boxing son, Thomas "Hitman" Hearns, meet Marvin Hagler in the ring. (By the way, Hearns went down in three rounds.) The cops to whom he provided information were on board with him taking the trip, figuring he'd have access to a gold mine of information.

Things continued like this, with Rick feeding info to the heat while enjoying the money they gave him for the tidbits on Curry and others. That is, until they had enough information to raid Curry's home. Several members of the Curry gang were indicted in the fall of 1987, and Johnny ended up spending 14 years in the clink.

And just like that, White Boy Rick's stock with the investigators sank like a hitman's gun in the Detroit River. No more visits from the Feds or the Detroit cops, and no more money.

Trouble is, Wershe had gotten addicted. Not addicted to drugs, but to the money. After the lifestyle and underworld status he had enjoyed, going back to the existence of the average teenager held little appeal for him. Eventually, he decided to line his pockets again doing the thing the cops taught him to do: selling drugs.

For a while, that satisfied his desire for status, even more so when he had, for a time, Cathy Volsen Curry on his arm. He was still only 16 and the powerful, stunning woman was nearly a decade his senior. She was also Detroit Mayor Coleman Young's niece, and Johnny Curry's wife.

Wershe was now risking his life in a whole new way. He wasn't telling on dangerous criminals, he was competing with them.

A particularly close call happened while he was riding in a car driven by a friend. As they waited at a red light, a van pulled up next to them. Rick saw the van's side door slide open and knew what was coming. A man raised a long gun and pointed it at him. Rick reached his leg over to the driver's side and stomped on the gas pedal, speeding away and narrowly escaping his own execution.

He continued to live with that threat until it all came crashing down after a traffic stop. On May 22, 1987, Detroit patrol cops pulled him over near his grandparents' home. Wershe was no stranger to the police, so they searched his car. When he ran to his grandparents'

house, police followed him. As they looked around the house, he slipped out the door with a bag. They caught up with him and found the bag contained 8000 grams, way more than one set of nostrils could use of cocaine.

That much dope pretty much spelled dealer, and even more unfortunate for Rick, it was way over the 650 grams that gave name to Michigan's new "650-lifer" law. That meant possession of 650 grams or more carried a mandatory life sentence. Rick was only 17, but he was tried as an adult.

White Boy Rick was now in court and all over the media.

Yet he figured his weighty connections in the police and FBI would speak up to help a teenager who made a mistake after giving them so much good information. Sure, he'd broken the law, but figured it was the officials who initially told him to wrap himself up in the drug business, hadn't they? Nothing doing. The FBI and the DPD refused to get involved in his defense. They didn't even want to acknowledge that they'd had a mere boy risk his life and future just to make their jobs easier.

Rick was on his own and the state of Michigan found Rick Wershe Jr. guilty and locked him up on the mandatory life sentence prescribed by the law. Still, Rick and those around him figured it wouldn't hold. Weeks turned to years as his old partners in crime-busting never rose up on his behalf. Though he and his family tried to remain optimistic, they watched Johnny Curry and others Rick had helped to convict get out on parole. As they sought appeals and waited, Rick Wershe became the longest-serving nonviolent offender ever in the state.

Wershe believed he may have been abandoned by officials who could help him because he also blew the whistle on

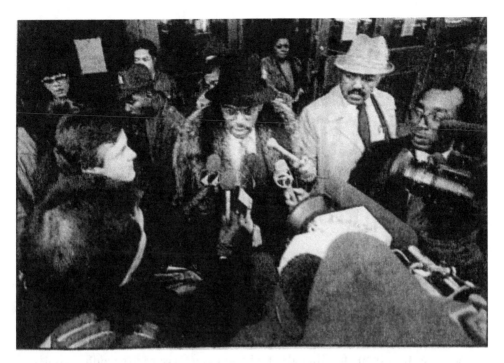

Richard Bell, Wershe's attorney, talks to reporters about the case. Wershe was painted as a drug kingpin, which many believe was a stretch. (Detroit Free Press, March 25, 2005)

crooked cops and "embarrassed a lot of people" while cooperating with an investigation of the police. It's even been alleged that former Detroit Police Chief, the late Gil Hill, wanted him dead.

Johnny Curry and the hitman who tried to kill him have both told the press they have no ill-will toward him and say they believe he should be freed. He became a cause celebre and has made some famous friends and advocates. Among them are rap singer Kid Rock and former Detroit Mayor Kwame Kilpatrick, himself serving time for perjury and obstruction of justice in relation to tax evasion and other corruption allegations.

Then, in 2005, Rick was convicted by the state of Florida for being involved in a car-theft ring, his sentence to be served after being released by Michigan. Wershe said he was trying to get a car for his sister.

After all that, however, Rick's story does have a happy ending.

The parole board in Michigan finally released him in 2017, though he is now wearing orange for the Florida penal system. Florida moved up his release date and he finally became a free man on July 20, 2020.

The White Boy Rick name still sticks, though he has told media he just wants to be called Rick these days. Whether he likes it or not, that name has become legend. It has graced numerous documentaries and news stories about him, and is the name of the 2018 movie in which his straight hair and gawky bearing was replaced by curly-headed Richie Merritt. Matthew McConnaughey played his dad.

LEGISLATING IMMORALITY: CAPITOL CORRUPTION TURNS DEADLY

WHERE: BETWEEN LANSING AND JACKSON
WHEN: 1945

STATE SENATOR WARREN G. HOOPER DROVE SOUTH ON M-99 PAST FARMS AND FIELDS AND THROUGH THE JANUARY COLD BETWEEN LANSING AND JACKSON. Hooper, a Republican, was on his way home to Albion on a Thursday night, looking forward to spending a quiet weekend there before getting back to the unpleasant task waiting for him back in Lansing.

That task was to testify before a grand jury investigating corruption in state government. Hooper had confessed to accepting a $500 bribe to sway his vote on a bill regarding horse racing. He'd agreed to testify in return for immunity from being charged for the bribe.

A passerby found the burned-out car on the side of M-99 on a bitterly cold January day in 1945. A slumped over figure in the passenger seat turned out to be the body of State Sen. Warren G. Hooper. Hooper had been driving home to Albion when another car ran him off the road. A man got out of the other car, and told Hooper to move over to the right-side of the front seat, then shot him three times in the face and head. Hooper's cigarette dropped from his lips and the upholstery and interior of the car went up in flames.

When police arrived and identified the dead man, they knew right away why he had been targeted. Hooper was to have returned to Lansing four days later to testify to a grand jury investigating corruption in state government. He had admitted to taking bribes to push changes in legislation affecting the horse-racing industry. Hooper had not yet revealed who had paid him the bribe, and his killing was likely timed to prevent that information from reaching the light of day.

The focus now shifted, from bribery and undue influence on lawmaking, to figuring out who killed Warren Hooper. If special prosecutor Kim Sigler could get to the bottom of that, he should have the other pieces of the puzzle. Sigler expected the probe to eventually point to Frank McKay, head of the state Republican party, who had been the subject of three unfruitful investigations since the beginning of the decade.

94

Police investigate items that might provide clues to State Sen. Warren G. Hooper's murder near Springport. He was found in this burned out car, and was shot in the head, as holes in his hat show. (Detroit Free Press, Jan. 16, 1988)

They received many leads, but the biggest break, seemingly, was when Sam Abramowitz turned state's evidence in return for immunity in the case. Abramowitz pointed the finger at Harry Fleisher, an associate of the Purple Gang, and believed to be the one who pulled the trigger in the Collingwood massacre (see page 100); as well as Fleisher's brother Sammy Fleisher, Detroit bar owner Mike Selik, and gambler Pete Mahoney.

The case went to trial in July, and Fleisher's lawyer argued that footprints in the snow leading up to Hooper's car actually matched Abramowitz's shoe size. He pointedly told the courtroom that it appeared Sigler gave immunity to the killer.

Still, the trial ended in convictions for Fleisher and his three co-defendants. They were sent to Jackson State Prison for up to five years on conspiracy charges.

Yet the trial failed to answer two major questions: who pulled the trigger, and who bankrolled the hit?

Investigations continued and were taken over by the new state police Commissioner Donald Leonard in 1947. Despite several leads, he decided there was not enough evidence to make a case against anyone. Seven years later, McKay supported Leonard's unsuccessful bid to unseat Democratic Gov. G. Mennen Williams. (Kim Sigler, also a Republican, had become governor in '47, and was off the case. He had appointed Leonard to head the state police.)

Now, some wondered if the shooter had been a Jackson inmate, who was let out specifically for the hit, and even used a prison vehicle to get there. All of it happened, supposedly, with the blessing of prison officials.

In 1987, author Bruce Rubenstein supported that theory in his book, "Three Bullets Sealed His Lips." The author pointed out that the official prison logs for vehicle use are missing for January 11, 1945, the day Warren Hooper died.

YOU CAN TRAIN A COW BUT YOU CAN'T COW A TRAIN

TRAINS WERE PRETTY SLOW BACK IN THE 1840s, THOUGH COWS WERE EVEN SLOWER. AND WHEN THE TWO MET, THE TRAIN USUALLY WON.

That was happening a lot on the Michigan Central Railroad line between Ann Arbor and Jackson, and it was getting expensive to the farmers who were losing all those heads of cattle. The farmers got mad.

In those days, there were no transcontinental rail lines, but rather a whole bunch of small, regional railroads. Michigan Central was one of those relatively small lines, operating just in the state of Michigan. The rail company formed in 1845, and within a couple of years, it was regularly sending trains on its east-west route through much of the southern part of the state, from Detroit, past Ann Arbor, and through Jackson, Marshall, Battle Creek and all the way to Niles on the Indiana border.

At first, the trains reached top speed at a mere 15 miles per hour, but that was enough to crush cows that wandered onto the tracks to graze. Michigan Central's stretch between Grass Lake and Jackson had a particularly high bovicide rate. That's because cattle owned by farmers in Leoni and Michigan Center often crossed the railroad tracks to feed in marshes on either side.

It was bad enough in the early days, but train technology moved quickly, and in a few years, the trains were chugging along at 30 mph. There were also a couple of safety features that hadn't been introduced yet, such as lights and whistles.

Rail passengers and employees were also in some danger. A collision with a large mammal whose job it was to get fat could derail and overturn a train in those days. An ox toppled one near Marshall, killing one crew member and spilling scalding water from the boiler onto another worker.

Farmers, though, felt the brunt of the losses, and they were getting fed up.

Abel Fitch took up the cause. Fitch was a farmer, but ironically, he grew peaches and didn't have any cattle. He was Michigan Center's first postmaster, and was no stranger to political activism. Fitch was also a member of the Underground Railroad, and was enthused to lead the farmers against the "aristocracy" of the railroad company.

Fitch assembled a group of cattle ranchers and together they wrote a letter to John Brooks, the superintendent of Michigan Central Railroad, demanding that the engineers drive more carefully, and that the company pay the farmers for their lost livestock. No way, was Brooks' reply. The cows were the farmer's responsibility, and the company wouldn't be paying a cent for some bumpkin's accidental ground beef.

The farmers didn't quit. They kept sending letters and making demands. Brooks responded by hiring butchers to inspect the bovine carcasses rotting along the rails, then accused the farmers of leading their sick and subpar cows onto the tracks to collect more money than they could ever hope to get by taking them to market.

Still, Brooks hoped to placate them by offering to pay half the market value for run-over cattle.

That offer was no good to Fitch. He stood on the steps of the American Hotel in Jackson and declared it "worthless humbug."

As the impasse continued, Fitch and followers met regularly in a tavern to plot their strategy, vent their spleens and tip back a few ales. Some of the farmers also resorted to dangerous vandalism. Once in a while, someone placed a log on the railroad tracks, which could derail a train if it hit it just the right way. If the conductor saw the log in time to stop for it, he'd ask crew and passengers to get out and move it. Others threw rocks or bricks at the trains as they passed, and some of them hit passengers. Word

started to get out, even in East Coast newspapers, that Michigan trains were unsafe because of the protests.

Then, on Nov. 19, 1850, the Michigan Central Railroad's freight depot in Detroit went up in flames. The fire reduced the sprawling complex to ashes, though nobody was injured.

Company officials figured the fire was set by the embittered farmers to avenge their loss of livestock. They couldn't prove it, though, so John Brooks hired Henry Phelps, an ex-prison guard, to infiltrate the farmers group and spy on them. Phelps pretended to want to buy some cattle and earned their trust. After mixing with them for a time, he reported back to railroad officials that Fitch and his friends plotted the fire, and used a slow-smoldering, foot-long device called a "match" that allowed an arsonist to plant it and get the hell out before it grew into flames. Phelps said they had enlisted the help of Detroit brothel- and saloon-owner George Washington Gay to plant the device. Gay admitted to receiving $150 from Fitch to start the fire.

Armed with that information, Brooks put together a posse that rode the rails out to Leoni and Michigan Center on April 19, 1851, to arrest 44 suspects, "about daylight in the morning and nearly every one in his night clothes," reported the Detroit Free Press. The article also accused the conspirators of devising a "torpedo" to blow up train engines and passenger cars as they drove over it.

The posse took the suspects, Fitch included, on a train back to Detroit to face trial and a hostile press and public. Their collective bond was set at $2 million, a mind-boggling sum at the time. That would be like $67 million today.

The posse crammed the suspects into one, large jail cell where they were under round-the-clock observation by guards contracted by the railroad. The defendants suffered filthy conditions and several of the accused became sick with ailments resulting from bad sanitation, such as dysentery. Also known as infectious diarrhea, that outbreak had to have made a bad living situation absolutely unbearable. Gay died within a month. Fitch, though he was a robust 43-year-old prior to his arrest, succumbed to the lousy conditions and "a broken heart" on Aug. 25, about halfway through the trial.

Fitch's body was taken back home to Michigan Center in Jackson County and greeted by dozens of carriages. An overflowing crowd of about 1,000 mourners and admirers filed into the Congregational Church or crowded around the doors and windows.

Even with the farmers' leader gone, the trial continued and garnered a lot of publicity. The accused also gained a powerful ally, as abolitionist U.S. Senator from New York, William Henry Seward,

argued in their defense. Seward, who would be appointed Abraham Lincoln's secretary of state a decade later, argued that the railroad company never proved the fire was set on purpose. He said the railroad may have pinned it on the farmers, so they could charge them with a crime away from their own home turf of Jackson County—which would likely have been friendlier to the defendants. Seward also argued that Fitch denied knowing Gay, and that Phelps, the spy and a convicted horse-thief, was the only witness who claimed they did know each other.

Besides, four months of trial and imprisonment had taken its toll on the accused, Seward concluded. "Want, and fear, and sorrow, have entered into all their dwellings. Their own rugged forms have drooped…. One of them—a vagrant boy—whom I found imprisoned here for a few extravagant words, that, perhaps, he never uttered, has pined away and died."

He concluded that the accusers would eventually have to face the same heavenly "tribunal" that Fitch was now standing before.

Yet despite Seward's powerful, two-day speech, the judge ended up convicting 12 of the defendants to between 5 and 10 years of hard labor.

Still, in the end, the farmers' complaints were heard. Within four years, the state legislature, led by future governor Austin Blair, passed laws to require trains to have warning bells and whistles to announce their approach. The law also mandated that the railroad companies put up fences to keep cattle off the tracks.

And from the cows' perspective, more of them could now live to be slaughtered another day.

Detroit's Purple Gang. While the Bernstein brothers remain the best-known of the gang's leaders, there were also several other prominent members.

DETROIT MOB FAMILIES

BERNSTEIN

The four Bernstein brothers—Abe, Raymond, Izzy and Joe—started their criminal careers as teenagers with vandalism, petty larceny and shaking down shop owners for money, in and around the Detroit Jewish ghetto where they grew up. Within a few years, they were sitting on top of the city's crime world as leaders of the Purple Gang.

By the end of the 1910s, the brothers were committing more serious crimes. Then, Prohibition gave them the opportunity to run booze in from Canada, as they were also performing armed robberies, running protection rackets and getting involved in gangland murders.

The 1920s saw them breaking into and corrupting unions, and starting the Cleaners and Dyers War (see page 42). The gang had nine main members, led by business manager Abe Bernstein, with his brother Raymond also playing a prominent part.

In addition to the Cleaners and Dyers War, the Milaflores Massacre of March, 1927 helped put them on the map. When a small band of Chicago and New

York criminals came to town and began kidnapping gamblers for ransom, they made the mistake of kidnapping one of the Purples. Retaliating, the Purples turned around and kidnapped one of theirs. They set up a supposed meeting at which three of the gang's men showed up with guns and shot up the out-of-town interlopers. The massacre was notorious for bringing the rapid-fire power of the Thompson submachine gun ("Tommy gun") to Motor City crime. Fred "Killer" Burke (see page 116) is said to have been the one operating the machine gun, but no concrete evidence was ever found to pin it on anyone. Shortly thereafter, Michigan banned the sale of submachine guns to the general public.

In addition to a few high-profile cases like that, the gang is believed to have murdered some 500 people during their heyday from the 1910s to the '30s.

The Purples' empire started to crumble in 1931, when they invited three of their former cohorts who wanted to branch off on their own to a sit-down at the Collingwood Estate. The three who were going rogue wanted to smuggle booze in from Canada on their own under the name The Little Jewish Navy, and to establish their own territory. The Purples saw that as a double-cross and as unwanted competition, so they had Sol Levine, who was friendly with both groups, set up the meeting at 1740 Collingwood Avenue (the manor is no longer standing). As the three Purples discussed the matter with the three "Navy" guys, Purple member Harry Fleisher stood up and opened fire on the rivals, killing all of them. When Fleisher and other Purples sped away, they left Levine there. The cops came and arrested him.

Levine had some valuable information for the police, so he turned state's evidence

and spilled his guts on the shooting and on other mob secrets. Harry Fleisher left Detroit so he wouldn't face charges. The Bernsteins and their gang, however, faced increased scrutiny from the cops and from rival gangs. Sicilian mobsters started competing for territory and taking out their men. In 1933, Sicilians executed Eddie Fletcher and Abe Axler, and other Purples showed up dead throughout the 1930s.

The Purples never ruled the city again, though Abe Bernstein lived until 1968, running a bookie operation.

(The Austin American, Aug. 29, 1963)

ZERILLI

When the Purples flamed out in the early '30s, Joseph Zerilli helped lead the Detroit Partnership, and elevate it to be the new dominant force in local crime, and an empire of loan-sharking, gambling, prostitution and murder. The official boss in the early 1930s was "Black Bill" Tocco, but he handed Zerilli the reins in 1936. Yes, Detroit Partnership is a boring name compared with Purple Gang, but then again it has lasted a lot longer, and is said to still be the dominant force in the southeastern Michigan underworld.

Joseph Zerilli led the organization until 1970, when he stepped aside so his son Anthony Zerilli could now run it. Anthony was part-owner of Hazel Park Raceway at the time, but then sold his share due to legal troubles. He was convicted in 1974 on charges related to corruption regarding his stake in a Las Vegas casino, and concealing his interest in said casino. His father Joseph then resumed as leader of the Partnership until his death due to health issues in 1977.

Anthony Zerilli was in prison in 1975, when former Teamsters leader Jimmy Hoffa disappeared after meeting with mob figures, but in 2013 he claimed to know the answer to the 38-year-old mystery of what happened to Hoffa. He said Hoffa was buried alive under a cement slab about 20 miles from where he was last seen, at a farm once owned by Jack Tocco, who had assumed control of the Partnership in 1977. The FBI excavated land around the farm, but found nothing.

Anthony Zerilli died in 2015.

TOCCO

William Vito "Black Bill" Tocco, Zerilli's confidante and brother-in-law came to Detroit from Sicily in 1912. He served in the U.S. Army and then joined the Eastside gang in bootlegging and other crimes. He hid his mob activities behind several businesses he owned, including a bakery, a produce supplier, a boat seller and an auto dealership. Both Tocco and Zerilli were arrested after Chester LaMare, a Westside mob boss, was shot to death in his home in March, 1931, but were released without ever being charged because police could not build a case against them.

Black Bill was a founding member of the Eastside Gang, and when the Purple Gang began to implode, he was instrumental in joining together the Eastside and Westside gangs. He led the new Detroit Partnership for five years before he put Zerilli at the helm and became an underboss, or second in command.

William Tocco and his wife, the former Rosalia Zerilli, spawned the criminally pedigreed Jack Tocco, who became a fixture in the Partnership.

Jack inherited a faltering organization when the elder Zerilli died in 1977, but he didn't officially take over until 1979. The FBI secretly filmed the ceremony in which he was officially made the boss. He was convicted on racketeering charges in the '90s, and served 11 months in a federal facility, though he continued to lead the crime organization until his death in 2014 at age 87, a reign of nearly four decades.

(Detroit Free Press, June 21, 1963)

GIACALONE

Anthony "Tony Jack" Giacalone was one of the two gangsters who met with Jimmy Hoffa on the day Hoffa disappeared in 1975, along with Anthony "Tony Pro" Provenzano, a capo in the New Jersey mob. If it weren't for Giacalone's connection to the Hoffa mystery, he might have remained just a shadowy figure who made occasional appearances in Detroit news stories. Instead, he rose to national notoriety. Of course, neither of the two Tonys—nor anyone else—has ever been charged in the enduring puzzle of Hoffa's departure.

A year earlier, in 1974, Tony Jack had been a suspect in the murder of businessman Harvey Leach, owner of the Joshua Doore furniture chain—a store well-known for its catchy commercial jingle. Leach was in financial trouble and had made the dicey decision to take out a loan from the mob. Giacalone had wanted Leach to sell the furniture retailer to a mob associate, and disagreements about that may have played into his murder.

The mid-1970s was a busy time for Tony Jack. He was convicted of tax evasion in '76 and received a 10-year sentence.

Tony Jack had joined the mob because he didn't want to be an Eastside working stiff like his old man. He worked the numbers racket, collected gambling debts and saw several charges and short jail stays in his rise in Zerilli's Detroit Partnership. He died in 2001, taking with him any knowledge he may have had about the Hoffa case.

His nephew, Jack "Jackie the Kid" Giacalone is currently the reputed Detroit Don, believed to have taken over in 2014 upon the death of Jack Tocco. Jackie became a capo, basically the third in command, in 1990, and has led gambling operations under Tocco. He's said to have gotten the nickname from his interest in legendary Western outlaw Billy the Kid, though he is said to hate the nickname. He's not an actual kid, as he turned 70 in 2020.

THE RISE OF JIMMY HOFFA

WHEN: 1930s–1975
WHERE: METRO DETROIT AREA AND UNION HALLS THROUGHOUT THE COUNTRY

NEARLY 50 YEARS AFTER HIS DISAPPEARANCE, JIMMY HOFFA IS PROBABLY BEST KNOWN FOR, WELL, DISAPPEARING.

Hoffa was a superstar of union leadership, someone who Attorney General Robert F. Kennedy called the second most powerful person in the United States in the early 1960s—Robert's brother, President John F. Kennedy, was the most powerful person. At the time, Hoffa was president of the International Brotherhood of Teamsters, the largest union in the country with 2.3 million members.

Hoffa spent his early childhood in Indiana. His father, a coal miner, died when he was seven, and his family moved to the Detroit area when he was 11. Jimmy dropped out of school at the age of 14 to help support his mother and his three siblings.

Jimmy got a job working at a warehouse for Kroger grocery stores. The work involved a lot of waiting around a dock for shipments to unload. Yet while the dock workers waited, they were off the clock. Their hourly pay only kicked in when the trucks arrived, and for as long as it took to get the groceries off the trucks and into the warehouse. If they didn't wait, they'd be replaced. That left the workers a lot of time to stand around together and grumble about not being paid for their time. They asked the bosses for better pay, better job security and better work conditions, but the management wasn't listening.

This culminated in a young Hoffa leading a short, but ingenious, strike. He used a large shipment of strawberries to get the point across. As perishables go, strawberries are more perishable than most. And when Michigan strawberries ripen, well, it's something people anticipate, as a marker of summer. Hoffa talked and moved with force and purpose, even at a five-and-a-half-foot-tall teenager.

As the trucks rolled in, the managers expected the waiting workforce to hop to it, as usual, and get them into refrigerated storage. Instead, the hourly workers demanded to negotiate with the big bosses. It didn't take long for the grocery chain's brass to realize that a

The puzzle of where Jimmy Hoffa's remains were dumped has had the FBI digging up several sites in Michigan over the decades. This site is one of the later searches, pointed to by an elderly mob figure in Oakland Township. Still, no bones, no sign. (Detroit Free Press, May 5, 1957)

fortune in strawberries was hanging in the balance, and they agreed to talk.

That launched Hoffa's legend and by age 19, he became the local leader of the union representing truck drivers and warehouse and dock workers. He worked hard at recruiting and negotiating, getting into the fray when the fists came out and sometimes knocking on the windows of parked trucks to make his pitch for union membership to sleeping drivers. Hoffa's charisma and tirelessness helped the union grow from 75,000 members in 1932 to 420,000 members by the end of the decade.

In the middle of that, he met his wife Josephine Poszywak at a laundry workers' strike, a fitting meet-cute for a budding labor leader.

As his position and his profile rose, Hoffa found that the union world sometimes intersected with the mob world. Sometimes businesses hired organized criminals as strikebreakers, to rough up demonstrating workers and let "scabs," or replacement workers, cross the picket line. Unions were also known to hire the mafia to influence recruiting, and for union members to vote how Hoffa wanted them to, and to persuade business owners to let the unions in. Or, if the owners paid the mob a regular fee, say $10,000 a month, the thugs would make sure the unions bothered other shops.

Hoffa grew increasingly comfortable working with the lawless, as he advanced his career and made real gains in workers' wages, benefits and standards of living.

He worked his way up from the regional level to leading the union statewide, and in 1952, he was named vice president of the Teamsters nationwide. The union continued to grow, but so did Hoffa's ties

Jimmy Hoffa stood 5'5" tall, but commanded perhaps the most powerful union in the United States, as the Teamsters controlled truckers, who in turn controlled the flow of commerce.

repeated negative stories about him in the Detroit News, so he bought a cadaver's head from the Wayne County morgue and sent it in a box to editor Martin Hayden.

Hoffa had risen far and fast, but of course, he wasn't aiming to top out at vice president. That's when his under-the-table loans bore big fruit for him. Hoffa had gotten to know John "Johnny Dio" Dioguardi, who helped him win over New York unions partly by creating "paper locals," or local chapters that only existed on paper, but threw their votes to Hoffa. And In 1957, Hoffa became president of the Teamsters.

But around that time Robert Kennedy, still a U.S. Senator, was targeting him for mob ties and corruption.

So, in 1960, when Kennedy's brother John F. Kennedy ran for president, Hoffa endorsed his Republican opponent, Richard Nixon, contrary to what most union leaders did then and now. And when Kennedy named his younger brother Robert as attorney general, RFK's resolve to bring down Hoffa intensified. Bobby Kennedy and others referred to his anti-corruption team as his "Get Hoffa Squad."

The two traded personal barbs. Hoffa spelled Kennedy's first name as Bobbie, the feminine way, to undermine his authority. And he supported the often-stated claim that the Kennedys' father, Joseph P. Kennedy Sr., had made his fortune in part by bootlegging illegal alcohol during Prohibition. Officially, the elder Kennedy made his money on

to the mob. He gave favors to get favors. He had ready access to the workers' pension fund, and loaned vast sums of cash from it to any friendly mobster who asked. Low-interest and no-interest loans from the union's vault, to which Hoffa had ready access, funded many shady real-estate deals. The loans also helped build Las Vegas casinos.

Adding to Hoffa's outside-the-law reputation, his associates sometimes committed atrocities on his behalf without his apparent knowledge. Hoffa's loyal right-hand man, Chuckie O'Brien, once saw that his boss was upset about

Police search Jimmy Hoffa's car after his 1975 disappearance. It was parked where Hoffa was last seen, but yielded no clues in the nearly half-century-old mystery. (Detroit Free Press, July 30, 2015)

Wall Street, in real estate, shipping and the entertainment industry, and some historians say the bootlegging claim is unsubstantiated.

In 1964, after JFK was assassinated, Bobby Kennedy's team convicted Hoffa on charges of fraud, conspiracy, attempted bribery and jury tampering. Hoffa spent three years trying to appeal the conviction. He exhausted his appeals in 1967 and was sentenced to 13 years in Federal prison.

Even prison couldn't dent Hoffa's popularity with the union members, though. The Teamsters re-elected him president in 1968, though he had to appoint an acting president to fill in while he was incarcerated.

In 1971, President Richard M. Nixon commuted Hoffa's sentence, with the stipulation that he stay out of union business until 1980.

Hoffa couldn't do that. He tried to have Nixon's order to stay away from the Teamsters reversed, but the courts upheld it. Still, he was working behind the scenes to get back into the Teamsters.

That's what led to the clandestine meeting that mob associates had scheduled with him in the parking lot of the Machus Red Fox restaurant on Telegraph Road in Bloomfield Township on July 30, 1975. And that, for many of us these days, is where the story of Jimmy Hoffa begins.

MAGDELAINE LAFRAMBOISE BREAKS THE FUR CEILING

WHERE: MACKINAC ISLAND, GRAND RIVER VALLEY, GRAND HAVEN & OTHER POINTS
WHEN: 1794–1897

MAGDELAINE LAFRAMBOISE WAS ONE OF THE MOST SUCCESSFUL FUR TRADERS IN THE GREAT LAKES REGION IN THE EARLY 1800s, AIDED BY HER FLUENCY IN ENGLISH, FRENCH, ODAWA AND OJIBWE LANGUAGES. But the shrewd and ambitious businesswoman really shined and got the credit she deserved only after her husband/business partner was murdered.

La Framboise was born Marguerite-Magdelaine Marcot, of an Odawa mother and a French father at Fort St. Joseph, an important trading post near what is now the Indiana border city of Niles.

In 1794, at age 14, she married the successful fur trader Joseph LaFramboise. A year later, she gave birth to their daughter, Josette, and 10 years after that, they had a son, Joseph Jr.

For 12 years, Magdelaine and Joseph were a fur-trading power couple. They spent their winters trading tools, weapons and other useful items to Native Americans for furs at one of their 20 posts throughout the western Lower Peninsula, from the Kalamazoo River to Grand Traverse Bay. Then, every spring, they made their way up to Mackinac Island to sell the furs they had collected throughout the season and to collect items to be traded for furs the next winter.

As a team, they made a name for themselves among the more successful fur traders in the Great Lakes region. Yet despite their business triumphs, disaster lurked around the corner.

In 1806, when they were heading south for their winter trading, taking a small boat down the Lake Michigan shoreline, they stopped to camp at the mouth of the Muskegon River. A Potawatomi man named Nequat asked Joseph for liquor. Joseph refused to give it to him, and that evening, as Joseph knelt to pray, Nequat stabbed him to death.

Tribe members brought Nequat to Magdelaine, offering her the chance to take revenge on him for killing her husband. Magdelaine could have had Nequat killed then and there, but she figured that executing him would not bring back her husband Joseph, so she forgave him.

Magdelaine LaFramboise's home on Mackinac Island was extensively renovated in the early 2010s and returned largely to its original style. It's now known as Madame LaFramboise Harbour View Inn and is next to Sainte Anne Church on Huron Street, where Magdelaine is buried.

She led her trading party to wrap up Joseph's body, and bury him in what is now Grand Haven, where the Grand River empties into Lake Michigan.

But Magdelaine wasn't done with the fur business. A true single working mother, she continued her travels, bartering from post to post, while also raising her 11-year-old daughter and infant son.

The fur business was a crowded field, yet Magdelaine achieved greater success than most of the men involved. She made up to $10,000 a year, which is the equivalent of more than $200,000 now, and was about 10 times what most independent fur traders made in a year at the time.

In 1820, Magdelaine was ready to call it quits. She sold her business, retired and moved to Mackinac Island full-time. About that time, tragedy struck, and her daughter Josette—who had married the brother of future U.S. President Franklin Pierce—died in childbirth, along with her newborn son. Magdelaine raised Josette's surviving daughter, and built a luxurious home on the island. She also built a school for Native American children and donated land on which to build Sainte Anne Catholic Church there. In recognition of her gift, when she died in 1847 at age 66, she was buried under the altar.

SOMEONE RIPPED HIM A NEW HOLE

WHERE: MACKINAC ISLAND, QUEBEC, ST. LOUIS
WHEN: 1822–1880

ALEXIS ST. MARTIN MADE A TREMENDOUS CONTRIBUTION TO MEDICINE BY GETTING SHOT IN THE STOMACH.

St. Martin was a fur trader from Quebec in his early 20s, hanging out and working at John Jacob Astor's American Fur Co. post on Mackinac Island, when an accidentally fired musket slug tore into his gut. The wound nearly killed him, but he hung on, as the U.S. Army had a presence on the island and Army surgeon William Beaumont gave him much of his attention.

The hole in his stomach did heal, though it didn't heal shut. His skin recovered in such a way that it left an unplanned orifice in his abdomen. Skin on the outside of his abdomen fused with tissue inside his stomach, forming what is called a fistula.

Dr. Beaumont examined him in fascination during his unusual recuperation. This accidental gas-hole that had formed on Alexis St. Martin was a window into the man's last lunch. In other words, it would allow Beaumont to observe human digestion in progress. No dissection of a cadaver could ever show him that, and in 1822, relatively little was known about the gastric system.

In one of Beaumont's first experiments, he tied a bit of food to a string and lowered it into St. Martin's new opening, straight into the stomach. When he pulled it out after a time, he saw that acid had begun to dissolve the food on the string. The amazed doctor did it again and wrote notes. He couldn't believe his luck. He'd happened upon a walking, talking, digesting laboratory that would allow him to make important additions to mankind's knowledge of the digestive tract.

Beaumont compared the stomach's action on meat versus veggies.

Fortunately for Beaumont and for science, St. Martin was a good sport about it. He submitted to several bouts of poking, prodding and food on a fishline, even though it sometimes gave him stomach pains.

Beaumont, however, had a lot more research to do. How quickly does milk solidify in our stomachs? What about collecting some of that stomach acid, to conduct tests on it outside of its natural environment?

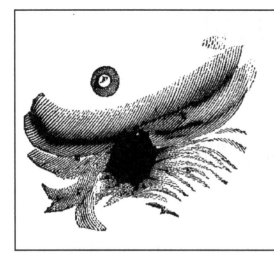

This engraving represents the appearance of the aperture with the valve depressed.

A A A Edges of the aperture through the integuments and intercostals, on the inside and around which is the union of the lacerated edges of the perforated coats of the stomach with the intercostals and skin.

B The cavity of the stomach, when the valve is depressed.

C Valve, depressed within the cavity of the stomach.

E E E F Cicatrice of the original wound.

F The nipple.

Dr. William Beaumont provided this illustration and explanation of Alexis St. Martin's bullet hole that became a permanent hole because of the unusual way in which it healed in his 1833 book, "Experiments and Observations on the Gastric Juice and the Physiology of Digestion."

The doctor had so much he wanted to research through Alexis St. Martin and he worried that the patient may want to get a life beyond his prodding and probing. Beaumont couldn't do his research without his guinea pig with the scenic sphincter.

Well, it just so happened that St. Martin lost his job at the fur trading post because of his injury. And, luckily for Beaumont, St. Martin couldn't read, and agreeably signed a contract that held him in servitude to the doctor for the next decade. Not only must he be a lab rat, but Dr. Beaumont put him to work with some fairly demanding chores. Of course, that was to monitor his response to physical strain, and if a winter's worth of wood got chopped and stacked as a result, so be it.

The doctor housed and fed the patient, but controlled him in return. By 1838, Beaumont had done enough research to publish Experiments and Observations on the Gastric Juice, and the Physiology of Digestion.

Still, Beaumont wanted to continue the study on his patient, whom he sometimes referred to in letters as "that old, fistulous Alexis." Beaumont wanted to tour with him and demonstrate his findings to other doctors and boards of doctors. Alexis St. Martin, however, was tired of being an object of research and curiosity. He wanted his life back.

St. Martin finally made it back to his native Quebec, and the Army reassigned Dr. Beaumont to a post in St. Louis, Mo. Beaumont sent word to Canada, trying to convince St. Martin to come and let him do more experiments and show him off. St. Martin had his relatives write a response, refusing the doctor's request.

The physician kept pleading with St. Martin to submit to more tests, until Dr. William Beaumont slipped on icy steps in St. Louis and died in 1853.

That wasn't the end of St. Martin being pestered about his unique hole, however. To the end of his life, other doctors and scientists pestered him, hoping he'd let them conduct their own tests on him.

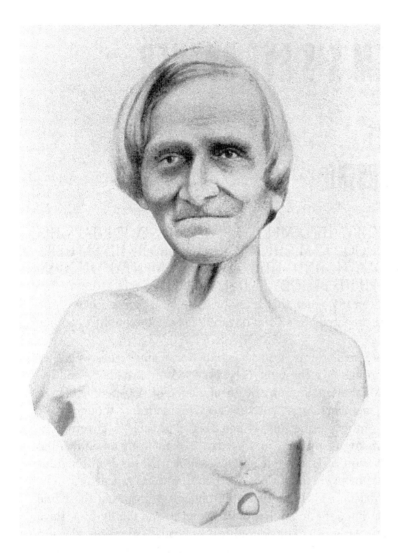

A portrait of Alexis St. Martin with his unusual wound below his left breast.

The only thing that stopped them from bothering Alexis St. Martin was when he died at the age of 78 in 1880.

St. Martin had often told his family that he didn't want any more invasive medical research, even after death. With this in mind, for several days after he perished, the family let the body lie out under the June sun, moon and crows. The result couldn't have been pleasant for anyone to see or smell. But at least his corpse wouldn't end up among the stinging chemical smells of a cold lab.

MEDICAL MAP

The American Fur Company Store & Dr. Beaumont Museum is at 7232 Market St., on Mackinac Island. This is the building in which Alexis St. Martin was shot, leading to Beaumont's ground-breaking discoveries on the human digestive system. The store sells items one might have found there 200 years ago, when the post was an important point of trade in John Jacob Astor's fur empire. In another room is a hands-on museum dedicated to Beaumont's work.

A Detroit-area hospital system was named after William Beaumont. The system is headquartered in Royal Oak, and there are no hospitals are named for Alexis St. Martin.

MALCOLM X'S EYE OPENER

WHEN: 1931
WHERE: LANSING

MALCOLM X KNEW HE'D MEET A BLOODY END. PERHAPS HIS TRAGIC CHILDHOOD IN MICHIGAN, SHATTERED BY HIS FATHER'S SUSPICIOUS DEATH AND HIS MOTHER'S MENTAL ILLNESS, FORESHADOWED HIS BLOODY END IN NEW YORK CITY.

"It has always been my belief, that I, too, will die by violence. I have done all that I can to be prepared," he said in dictating his autobiography to author Alex Haley.

Infamously, the civil rights leader's prediction came true when 13 bullets ripped through his chest on Feb. 21, 1965, at Broadway and W. 165th Street in Manhattan in front of an audience of 400 people. Three Nation of Islam members were convicted of his murder, though their motives and other questions—including possible government involvement—remain a mystery to this day. X had been an influential member of the Nation of Islam, but had left and started his own religious group, and it's unknown whether or not that played into his murder.

He was born Malcolm Little in 1925, but ended up dropping the name Little as an adult. Since the name had been given to the family by a slave owner generations earlier, he considered it a reminder of oppression and servitude.

Judge magazine, Aug. 16, 1924

His mother, Louise, and father, the Rev. Earl Little, both worked and fought for Black causes. Louise grew up in Grenada, having been conceived when a White man raped her mother. Earl, a Baptist minister from Georgia, spread the teachings of Jamaican political leader Marcus Garvey as well as the Christian Bible. Garvey urged Black people to stand up for their rights and rely on themselves, rather than on White society. Louise met Earl when she joined the Universal Negro Improvement Association, where she assumed the role of spreading news of their works to other African American rights groups.

Violence shaped Malcolm's world as far back as the womb.

When Louise was pregnant with Malcolm, the Littles and their children lived in Omaha, Nebraska. The families enjoyed a higher economic status than

Malcolm X snaps a picture of legendary boxer Cassius Clay, who later changed his name to Muhammad Ali, far right, at a lunch counter.

many Black families in the mid-1920s because of Earl's work as a preacher. Yet that relative prosperity—and their penchant for speaking their minds— also put them in the cross-hairs of White supremacists.

One night when Louise was pregnant with Malcolm, several Ku Klux Klansmen rode up on horseback to the Littles' house, waving shotguns and rifles and demanding that the rabble-rousing minister come out. Earl was not there, though, since he was in Milwaukee on a speaking engagement, so the visibly expectant mother Louise bravely stood at the door between the angry mob and her children inside. Once they realized she was telling the truth, that Earl was out of town, they rode around the outside of the house, smashing in windows to terrorize the family inside and send a threatening message to the father.

After Earl returned, the family left Omaha for Milwaukee, for a time, and eventually moved to Lansing. But hate, violence and heartache followed them.

When they got to Michigan's capital city, they bought a house in a middle-class neighborhood known as Westmont on the northwest side of the city. Their White neighbors resented them being there, and the land company that had built the subdivision decided that the development should remain exclusively White. The land company sued the family to get them out of there and to keep Westmont segregated and found a sympathetic ear in Ingham County Judge Leland Carr. Carr, who would later become chief justice of the state supreme court, ruled that the Littles had to move out. Sure, they could continue to own the house. They just couldn't live there.

They never got the chance to move.

One of four-year-old Malcolm's first memories was waking up at that house to the searing orange glow of fire and the sound of guns firing. His father was

The stage where Malcolm X was shot to death, with bullet holes in the wall circled.

firing the shots as the men who had apparently started the fire ran away. Earl figured they were members of Michigan's Black Legion, a hate group of White men much like the KKK. They dressed in robes and identity-concealing hoods and spread terror throughout Detroit and southern Michigan in the 1920s and '30s. The main difference between them and the more famous Klan was that they wore black instead of white.

Earl's growing bitterness festered as he watched White police and firemen stand at a distance and let the house burn to the ground, according to Malcolm's account.

Uprooted once again, the Littles moved across town to the south side of Lansing, to an area that was rural at the time but has since grown to be part of the city. They increased their self-reliance there, raising chickens and planting vegetables. It was far from an idyllic home life, though, as the parents ruled with flaring tempers and heavy hands, as if taking out on their children the cruelties they suffered from society. In Malcolm's words, their father was "belligerent toward all of the children except me. The older ones, he'd beat almost savagely if they broke any of his rules, and he had so many rules, it was hard to know them all."

Still, Earl was his father, and the way he met his end two years after the fire tore the family apart.

On Sept. 28, 1931, Earl had an argument with Louise and ended the quarrel by tearing the head off a rabbit for dinner then throwing it at the feet of his wife. That was the last time the family saw him alive. He was found late that night, his body sliced nearly in half from a trolley on Lansing's east side. The Lansing State Journal wrote that he was apparently running to catch the trolley,

Louise and Earl Little in an undated photo.

when he fell under the wheels. The driver said he didn't see Little until after he fell under the steel wheels. Police ruled his death an accident, though African Americans were never satisfied with that apparently hasty determination. Earl's skull was bashed in, leading many to suspect he was beaten and then thrown under the streetcar to make it look like an accident.

By the end of the decade, Louise suffered a nervous breakdown and was committed to Kalamazoo State Hospital about the time Malcolm hit his teenage years. He went to Flint to live for a while before making his way to Harlem in New York City. Once there, he turned to drug dealing, robbery and pimping, before a prison sentence set him on the path to religious and political activism.

However much his formative years in Lansing led to his life path and violent death is for someone else to decide. Certainly, his parents' activism influenced him to speak out on politics and injustice. Then again, seeing that someone apparently got away with murdering his father must have had an impact, as well.

MURDER MAP

There's a historical marker at the corner of what is now Martin Luther King Jr. Blvd. and Vincent Court on Lansing's south side. It's at a site where Malcolm X once lived when he was growing up as Malcolm Little. The site now houses condominiums among a commercial district. Lansing residents fought for years to have the marker erected there.

Several miles northeast of there, at the intersection of East Michigan Avenue and Detroit Street, is the area where his father died. There are no longer trolley tracks there. As of the summer of 2019, a handmade marker stood by a parking lot at the intersection, paying tribute to Rev. Earl Little.

There is also a Malcolm X Street in Lansing, which runs for a couple miles parallel to Business Route 496, to honor the troubled Michigan roots of the boy who became a crusader for African American rights.

ST. VALENTINE'S GUN FINDS A HOME WITH MICHIGAN SHERIFF

WHERE: ST. JOSEPH
WHEN: 1929

THE ST. VALENTINE'S DAY MASSACRE IS ARGUABLY THE MOST INFAMOUS MOB HIT EVER. On the holiday of love, 1929, in a gritty Chicago garage, four gunmen working for Al Capone lined up seven members of Bugs Moran's Northside gang and sprayed them with machine gun fire. They left their bodies oozing blood on the garage floor.

So how did two of the Tommy Guns used in this Prohibition-era vendetta end up in the hands of the Berrien County Sheriff's Department? The answer involves the murder of a cop right in front of a throng of Christmas shoppers.

It was December 14, 1929, 10 months to the day after the sensational bloodbath in Chicago. Fred "Killer" Burke was cooling his heels in St. Joseph, living under an assumed name just south of town. Burke was a mob-associated trigger man who had ties to the Capone gang and the Purple Gang. He had been clever enough, so far, to never leave damning evidence behind, yet his name was tossed around among cops puzzling over the St. Valentine's Day job. He was also a suspected shooter in the Purples' Miraflores massacre two years earlier in the Motor City.

Nowadays, though, he lived quietly in a Lakeshore Drive home with a woman friend named Viola, while people in town came to know him as wealthy oil man Fred Dane. He had a good thing going until he unraveled his own ruse on that slushy Saturday evening by having a bit too much to drink before he slipped in behind the wheel of his Hudson. As he drove along feeling the alcoholic glow, his car drifted onto the wrong side of Lakeshore traffic and he sideswiped another car driven by local farmer F.L. Kool. They stopped and saw the dent in Kool's car and argued about who should pay. By some accounts, Kool even told Fred he could take care of the whole thing if he paid him $5. Yeah. A lousy fin. Granted, that would be like more than $70 today, but still not enough for even the smallest dent in a car.

Burke refused to take that easy-out. He angrily got in his car and drove away. Kool jumped in his vehicle and followed him, oblivious to the fact that he was chasing down a guy who was suspected of robbing several banks and killing a whole bunch of dangerous people. Burke just wanted to get out of there without having to talk to the cops.

116

St. Valentine's Day Massacre occurred 10 months to the day before Fred Burke blew his cover in St. Joseph. When police searched Burke's home after he shot a local police officer, they found machine guns that had been used in the infamous mob massacre.

Kool wasn't going to let him get away, though, and kept after Burke trying to get him to pull over. As they passed through downtown St. Joseph, they came to a red light where Officer Charles Skelly happened to be on foot patrol. Kool yelled out his window to the policeman, saying that sonofagun in the Hudson had hit him and was trying to get away. Skelly told the two to go to the police station and work it out. Burke figured he'd just drive away and lose Kool and the cop: it's not like the officer could chase him.

Before he could drive away, however, Officer Skelly surprised him by hopping onto the running board of Burke's car to direct him to the police station.

Burke pulled a .45 out of his door pocket and blasted the first shot into the policeman, blowing him away from his car, as holiday shoppers' eyes widened at the sudden violence. Officer Skelly tried to get up, when he caught another shot in his side and a third in his back. He fell to the cold pavement. He put up a hand and a knee to push himself up, feebly, then fell again. Burke peeled off and bystanders found a nearby car to drive Skelly to a doctor.

Burke kept going, until he ran off the road on a curve and wrecked his right-side wheels. He took off on foot, running for a ways, keeping his eyes out for a car he could steal. When he saw a car idling at a stop sign, he heaved the door open and pulled his gun on the man behind the wheel. Burke told the man to drive south, and as he got close to his home, he told the man to stop. He got out of the car and told the driver to stick around until he checked out his driveway for cop cars. As soon as Burke stepped away from the car, the unwitting chauffeur stepped on it, getting snow and trees between himself and the guy with the lopsided moustache who wouldn't stop waving the handgun around.

Burke approached his home with caution. He figured that with all those shoppers witnessing the shooting, someone might have identified him as Mr. Dane, that oil magnate. He figured there was a good chance of a car or two already making it there, but was surprised to see a swarm of cars, badges and guns.

As he skulked among the trees, police saw his silhouette in the distance. He disappeared into the woods before they could get to him. He made his way to the home of a neighbor who had no idea of the commotion in town. Burke asked him for a ride to the town of Coloma, northwest of St. Joseph. The neighbor agreed and started driving him eastward on main roads. Burke asked him to get on the back roads to take an indirect route. That sounded suspicious, so the neighbor started wondering how he could get out of doing this neighborly favor. Fortunately, the fugitive asked him to stop at a drug store. When Burke went inside, his second ride of the night drove off.

Back at the "Dane" residence, police gathered up firearms and other evidence, and questioned Viola, the woman claiming to be the oil man's wife. As if burrowing, she pulled a mink coat around herself. The coat was a gift from Burke, and nicer than anything she could have afforded on her wages and tips as a hairdresser in Chicago. Fred was a sweet man when he wasn't drinking, she told the cops. No, she didn't have any photos of him, she said. He hated to have his picture taken. "Didn't you think that was

Fred "Killer" Burke. The "Killer" wasn't just a nickname, it was a job description. Burke is believed to have pulled the trigger on gangland murders in Detroit and Chicago.

peculiar?" a detective asked. She pulled the mink tighter and shrugged.

As she answered questions, other detectives emptied closets and drawers and boxes. They found several guns which were definitely not the deer-hunting kind. Two of the firearms were Thompson submachine guns. Firing 700 rounds per minute, the Txfommy gun had made a bloody splash during the Great War (what they called World War I until the sequel in the 1940s). The Tommy Gun's infamy grew as the '20s gangsters used it when they needed to get the job done definitively and make a statement. Viola said she didn't know about the guns, or the $350,000 in stolen bank bonds they had just found hidden in a clothing closet of her bedroom.

Police also found evidence of Fred Dane's true identity. They would soon

118

The Thompson Submachine Gun advertised as the "anti-bandit gun" was also used by bandits in high-profile murders. This brochure marketed the "Tommy Gun," for law enforcement, but the bad guys were already well aware of its power to get the job done and make a major statement.

learn that Fred "Killer" Burke started out in St. Louis, where he was a member of a gang known as Egan's Rats. In the mid-1920s, he moved to Detroit, where he "painted houses" with the blood of some of the Purple Gang's enemies. He was suspected of the 1927 Miraflores massacre, in which three hitmen sprang out of an apartment building fire escape, ambushed three foes of the Purples and sprayed them with bullets, introducing machine-gun warfare to the Motor City underworld and putting an exclamation point on the gang's gruesome legend. And, they would learn of his move to Chicago and possible, and many believe probable, involvement in that slaughter in the garage back in February.

As police continued to grill Viola and gather up evidence at the house, their friend and colleague Chuck Skelly lay dying on an operating table at the St. Joseph Sanitarium. Skelly's sister, Olga Moulds, sat beside him, praying and fighting back tears. As surgeons were about to have him sedated so they could try to remove the slugs from his body, he told her, "You had better kiss me goodbye now. I'll never pull out." His prediction was right, shattering Olga's heart.

While she arranged the funeral for her 25-year-old brother, now a dead hero, the Berrien County Sheriff's detectives picked up the phone and dialed the Chicago police. Yeah, they knew Burke.

119

A real bad egg. He ran with Capone and had erased more than a few of Scarface's enemies.

The Chicago police perked their ears up when they heard about the Tommy Guns. They'd never been able to find the tommies used in the massacre, but they had plenty of shells and slugs from the murder scene.

Now, it just so happened that Dr. Calvin Goddard was blazing trails at that time in the new science of ballistics at Northwestern University. Taking the two weapons from Burke's stash, the local police drove them to Goddard's lab. He fired the guns into a soft target and compared those bullets to others found at the massacre site.

They matched, meaning that Burke had been hiding the St. Valentine's Day Massacre guns. Now, police in Chicago and St. Joseph wanted to get hold of Burke more than just about anything.

As some police searched for him, others continued to dig into his past, including his stay in southwestern Michigan. They built a case against him in Skelly's murder, asking shopkeepers again if a photo of Burke matched up with the wide-faced, mustached man they knew by the name of Dane.

"That's Dane, all right," confirmed several businesspeople, including the owner of a dry cleaning shop who had suffered a humiliating tirade from "Dane" after the cleaner printed the customer's name inside the clothes he'd dropped off there.

Leads thinned out and Burke was still nowhere to be found. He had slipped into thin air, despite the early mishaps on the night of his St. Joseph getaway.

The next break finally came 15 months later and about 500 miles away.

Burke had made his way to northern Missouri—to the town of Green City—where he was living under the alias Richard F. White. He'd wooed and married 20-year-old nurse Bonnie Porter and the two of them took up residence in a farmhouse.

Unfortunately for Burke, a truck driver who lived nearby named Joseph Hunsacker thought it was odd that Mr. White never seemed to go anywhere, yet seemed to dress like he had money. Hunsacker read a lot of true-crime magazines, so when he had a hunch that something wasn't right about his neighbor, he grabbed a stack of them and started thumbing through for photos of gangsters. One of them, a guy named Fred "Killer" Burke, bore a striking resemblance to his new neighbor. He picked up a phone and dialed the police.

On the morning of March 26, 1931, Fred Burke woke up to find uniformed police officers standing over him in his bedroom. They told him that the place was surrounded, and besides that, Burke realized he couldn't reach his gun, hanging in a holster near the bed, anyway. Burke threw on some clothes and the cops threw on the cuffs and led him into a squad car.

The mob assassin was wanted in several states, so Missouri police notified authorities in Illinois, Michigan, and other states where he was suspected of murders and robberies. The governor of Missouri gave preference to Michigan's claim on him, as their case against him in Skelly's killing was particularly solid. A heavily armed police caravan started out for St. Joseph.

When they arrived on the evening of March 30, Burke took a hurried perp walk into the courthouse as a phalanx of armed officers kept the curious throngs at bay, fearing someone would want to shoot him or help him escape.

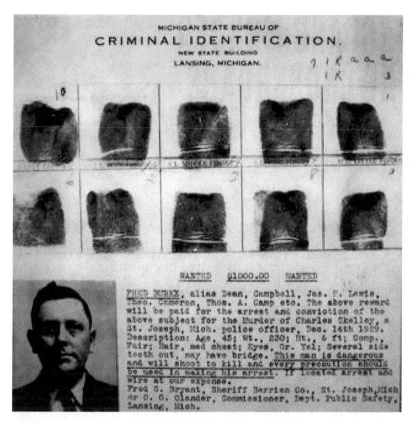

Fred Burke's mugshot and fingerprints taken at his arrest for the murder of Officer Charles Skelly.

Because Burke was drunk when he killed Skelly, he was able to plead guilty to a charge of second-degree murder, hoping he would eventually be paroled. He received a life sentence and heard the steel doors clang shut on him at Marquette State Prison.

Corrections officers said he was a model prisoner. He raised canaries to pass the time in his cell—a curious choice for someone who had long feared the mob would clip his wings for fear that he might sing.

In the end, he did serve a life sentence, but it was only nine years. He died of a heart attack in his bed on July 10, 1940.

But what about his part in the St. Valentine's Day Massacre? It happens that neither Burke nor anyone else ever faced charges for that crime. While there's a decent case to be made for Burke being one of the shooters, it has never been proven beyond a doubt. Investigators believe some 25 people participated in the planning and execution of the, well, execution.

Astonishingly, not one of them ever pointed a finger or gasped a deathbed confession, and the Tommy Guns in the legendary crime remain a curiosity at a southwestern Michigan sheriff's department.

A GANGLAND MURDER
AT THE CROSSROADS

WHERE: CLARE
WHEN: 1938

ON A SATURDAY NIGHT IN MAY, 1938, ISAIAH LEEBOVE STROLLED INTO THE HOTEL DOHERTY, THE FOUR-STORY BRICK BUILDING IN THE CENTER OF DOWNTOWN CLARE. Leebove's wife Enid had asked him to go to town and get her some ice cream.

Little did Leebove know, a disgruntled former business partner was watching him and had murder on his mind.

That former partner was Jack Livingston, known as "Tex" by friends and associates because he grew up in Houston. He saw Leebove step into the door that led to the hotel restaurant, so he ran up to the room in the Doherty in which he'd been living. Livingston picked up the .38-caliber handgun he kept there, stuffed it in his clothing and went down to the restaurant.

Livingston found a booth near the table where Leebove had sat down to chat with a fellow lawyer, Byron Geller, and his wife Elizabeth.

Leebove and Geller had a friendly relationship as they were both attorneys, though they had different backgrounds. Geller had been a newspaper reporter in Windsor, Ontario, then assistant attorney general for the state of Michigan, and now had a private practice in Clare.

Leebove, on the other hand, had practiced law in New York City and had represented some heavy hitters in organized crime, including mobsters like Salvatore Spitale and Irving Bitz—go-betweens in the ransom negotiations for the Lindbergh baby. He also represented Arnold Rothstein, a gangster involved in gambling who is believed to have helped fix the 1919 World Series. His legal services extended to members of Detroit's Purple Gang as well. Leebove claimed he had left his practice in New York and came to Clare because he was tired of working for "scum." Others have said he came because he felt the heat of the law breathing down his neck in the Big Apple.

As Livingston sat at the booth hearing Leebove talk and laugh with the Gellers, he felt the heavy gun at his side. He'd been considering what he'd wanted to do for some time now.

Livingston and Leebove's association started a few years prior after oil was discovered in central Michigan and the two men started drilling and investing near Clare. They joined forces and their venture eventually became Mammoth Producing & Refining Co., which grew into the largest oil company east of the Mississippi.

But they often argued bitterly over how to run the company. Due to their volatile relationship, Livingston eventually left the company that had made both him and Leebove a lot of money. Leebove was still doing well, having built a luxurious log home on the Tobacco River that he called Tobacco Ranch. He and Enid, a former showgirl from Canada, entertained the wealthy and powerful at the ranch, including ex-Gov. William Comstock, whose campaign he helped bankroll.

Livingston, on the other hand, had squandered his earnings and was now hurting for cash. His hatred of Leebove ate at him, or as he said later, "He ruined my soul." He claimed his former partner had cheated him out of everything. And he had convinced himself that his former associate had used his friendship with Meyer Lansky—a well-known New York crime figure—to order a hit on him.

Now, sitting in the restaurant a few feet from the object of his resentment, Livingston figured he had thought about it enough. He stood up, walked over to Isaiah Leebove's table, pointed the .38 at him and began firing. The shots blew Leebove off his chair, as a stunned Geller stood up. Leebove writhed on the floor, gasping, "Jack, Jack, why?"

In the sudden melee, Geller noticed that he too had taken two bullets in his leg. Jack "Tex" Livingston walked over to Harry Wehrly, the assistant manager of the hotel, handed him his gun and went upstairs to his rented room, accompanied by a bellhop, to quietly wait for the police.

A doctor heard of the shooting and ran to the hotel within minutes, only to declare Isaiah Leebove dead at the

(The News Palladium, May 16, 1938)

Isaiah Leebove was buying ice cream for his wife when former business associate Jack Livingston shot him to death in the middle of a cocktail lounge.

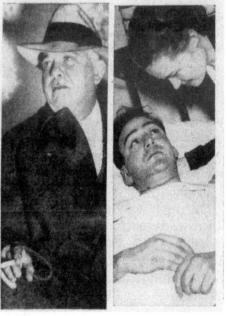

(Detroit Free Press, May 17, 1938)

Jack Livingston, left, who shot Leebove and his other, unintended victim, Byron Geller, who was injured by a stray bullet. His wife is visiting him in the hospital.

The Doherty Hotel in Clare, where the murder occurred on the bottom floor. The Leebove shooting is still a source of curiosity to hotel visitors. (Lansing State Journal, May 16, 1938)

age of 42. The chaotic crowd was soon joined by Enid, who had heard that her husband was shot and sped downtown to the Doherty. She saw her lifeless husband and collapsed, sobbing.

Livingston sat in his room dictating to the bellhop a message for his father, expecting the police at any minute. He went with them peacefully as they led him to their car and to the county jail in Harrison.

Livingston stood trial for the murder. There was no question and no argument that he had indeed shot a bullet through Leebove's heart, in cold blood and in a restaurant in front of several witnesses. Yet his defense convinced the court that he had acted in a state of temporary insanity.

The jury acquitted Livingston, though he was committed for a short time to a northern Michigan mental institution. He died of a drug overdose ten years later in New Jersey.

The shooting remains a curiosity to this day, particularly to those visiting the Doherty Hotel. The mob ties are often part of the narrative, as they should be. Detroit and New York gangsters had dealings with Mammoth and other connections in the local oil industry. And Leebove's ties with Lansky certainly played into Livingston's deadly paranoia.

But in the end, it appears to have been a crime committed out of very personal paranoia and animosity.

RIGHTEOUS CRIMINALS AND THE UNDERGROUND RAILROAD'S LAST STOP

WHERE: MARSHALL, SCHOOLCRAFT, BATTLE CREEK, ANN ARBOR, YPSILANTI, PLYMOUTH, DETROIT, PORT HURON AND SEVERAL OTHER STOPS IN SOUTHERN MICHIGAN
WHEN: PRE-CIVIL WAR 1800s

ESCAPED SLAVES TREKKED UNDER THE STARS TOWARD MIDNIGHT. Guides led them through the night from house to farm to church, all through southern Michigan after having mostly come up through Indiana. Midnight, the code name for Detroit, was their last destination before freedom.

During this last leg before finding new lives in Canada, the runaway slaves may have stayed in a secret room under the altar at Second Baptist Church. They may have hidden in a barn that housed carriages. If they had an opportunity to look across the river from Midnight, they would see a symbolic dawn of a life in which they could presumably work for a wage they could take to the home of their own choosing. They would no longer have to worry about someone selling their children or spouse, sending them to some undisclosed location.

In fact, a lot of people made the daring voyage for just that reason; to avoid having a family member sold away to who knows where. Among such families were that of Adam and Sandra Crosswhite. They fled Kentucky, where they had been enslaved to owner Francis Giltner, when they learned in August, 1843, that Giltner intended to sell one of the Crosswhites' children. The family fled the Giltner farm and made it across the Ohio River into Indiana, with the help of Underground Railroad volunteers. Eventually, they made it to southern Michigan. They didn't head to Canada right away. For a while, they settled in Marshall, where several abolitionists and former slaves lived.

The Crosswhites enjoyed a few years of peace there, though Kentucky slave owners were banding together more and more to regain their runaway investments. The Kentuckians sent spies to Michigan, to pose as abolitionists

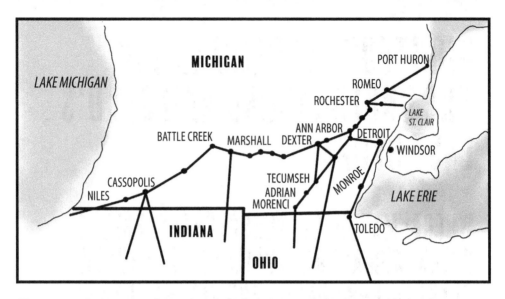

There were at least seven paths winding through the state in the Underground Railroad system, and 200 or so stops in operation between the 1820s and the end of the Civil War. The stops included private homes, churches, barns and carriage houses.

and find out whose slaves were hiding out where. One spy recognized the Crosswhites and sent word back to the Giltner family.

Francis Giltner sent his nephew Francis Troutman to lead a posse of four slave catchers on a mission to return the farmer's "property," the Crosswhites, and return them to his farm in the Ohio River Valley.

When Troutman and company found the Crosswhites' home, they broke through the door. Troutman burst in, waving a gun around and telling the family to come with him. The family wasn't about to go with them, and there was a bit of a standoff. Adam Crosswhite sneaked out the back door to run and get the sheriff, and neighbors began to surround the house, aware of what was going on.

Inside, Troutman was threatening and trying to convince Sandra to give up and go back to a life of imprisoned servitude. Mrs. Crosswhite was not going to budge and Troutman suggested, well, OK then, how about just the children?

Word of the legal kidnapping party spread around town and soon there were 150 or so people outside ready to come to the Crosswhites' aid if anybody tried to take the family away. But with nothing happening either way, one small group tried to barge into the house to help the family get rid of the unwanted visitors. In the melee, Troutman assaulted one of the townspeople. Well now, up to that point, he hadn't done anything illegal but trespass. That was in the process of trying to return runaway slaves, which was not only legal, but encouraged by law. But now, Deputy Sheriff Harvey Dixon, who had just arrived, could arrest this out-of-towner for assaulting a local resident.

The Crosswhite family had won that round, but the Crosswhite family figured they just may try again. So, with the help of their neighbors, they left Marshall in a covered wagon, headed for Midnight. When they got there, they took a boat across the river to Canada.

Giltner sued the residents of Marshall in federal court to be paid for his

CAUTION!!

COLORED PEOPLE

OF BOSTON, ONE & ALL,

You are hereby respectfully **CAUTIONED** and advised, to avoid conversing with the

Watchmen and Police Officers of Boston,

For since the recent **ORDER OF THE MAYOR & ALDERMEN**, they are empowered to act as

KIDNAPPERS

AND

Slave Catchers,

And they have already been actually employed in **KIDNAPPING, CATCHING, AND KEEPING SLAVES.** Therefore, if you value your **LIBERTY**, and the *Welfare of the Fugitives* among you, *Shun* them in every possible manner, as so many *HOUNDS* on the track of the most unfortunate of your race.

Keep a Sharp Look Out for KIDNAPPERS, and have TOP EYE open.

APRIL 24, 1851.

127

"A Ride for Liberty—The Fugitive Slaves" by Eastman Johnson, Brooklyn Museum

financial loss from the Crosswhites fleeing. A jury in Detroit later awarded him $4,500 in losses and court fees, which would be around $146,000 today. Detroit abolitionist Zachariah Chandler paid most of the fine and the Crosswhites moved back to Marshall after the Civil War.

Some slaves made the journey on their own without the help of the Railroad, like Thornton and Lucie Blackburn, who fled Kentucky in 1831, when they learned that their owner planned to ship Lucie to New Orleans and sell her. The two slaves dressed in their Sunday finest and stuffed forged freedom papers into their pockets. They convinced a steamboat captain to board them for the short ride across the river to Cincinnati and the free north.

Well, freer than the South, but that was not a high bar for people who had been property. This was two decades before Congress' 1850 Fugitive Slave Act, a pre-Civil War "compromise" between the North and South, ruling that Northerners had to return any slaves to their owners if they knew of them. Abolitionists grimly referred to it as the "Bloodhound Bill." As an unintended consequence, it also inspired the political organization and growth of abolitionists, and eventually to the Republican Party. Even in the years before this "Bloodhound Bill" was enacted, bounty hunters roamed the free states looking for runaway slaves to kidnap and sell back to their old masters.

In the 1830s, there were already plenty of White people all along the route who were more than willing to turn in escaped slaves. And 260 miles from Kentucky, after they arrived in Detroit, someone recognized them and reported them to their owners. They were arrested and tossed in jail (which was where the Skillman Branch of the Detroit Public Library is now). When two women visited Lucie, saying they wanted to pray with her, they sneaked her out of the jail.

Later, Thornton was brought to the jail in chains, and 200 or so people, Black and White, demanded his release. They led him to a cart and took him across the river to Canada.

Southern Michigan had several Underground Railroad routes running through it, depending on which point of Indiana or Ohio the escapees came through. Most of them led to Detroit as the last stop before Canada, though Port Huron and Sault Ste. Marie did see some crossings as well. Dozens of homes, barns, carriage houses and other buildings were used, and people too numerous to list also helped out at various posts. A vast number of the White people engaged in the system were Quakers, as the church was an early and strong voice in the abolitionist movement.

Here are some other people and places involved in the Underground Railroad's Michigan leg, roughly from west to east, since that's the way most of the one-way traffic ran:

Chain Lake Baptist Church in Cassopolis was one of the first Black congregations in the state and took a leading role in organizing African Americans against slavery. Nearby, the Brownsville School was used in the Underground Railroad during the 1850s. The school also had the rare distinction at the time of educating Black and White children together. And the old Cass County Courthouse, since replaced by a newer building, was the site of a group of Quakers facing down a group of Kentucky slave catchers in 1847.

"Station master" James E. Bonine hid runaway slaves in the carriage house on his property in the village of Vandalia. The home has been renovated in recent years.

In the Kalamazoo County town of Schoolcraft stands a Greek Revival style house at 613 E. Cass St., that hid hundreds of runaway slaves between 1843 and the end of the Civil War. Dr. Nathan M. Thomas and his wife Pamela Brown Thomas hid slaves who'd come up through Indiana, and Pamela estimated in her journals that they'd helped 1,000 to 1,500 slaves over the years. Dr. Thomas was a founding member of Michigan's Republican Party.

Most of the slaves brought to the Thomas home came from Zachariah Shugart, a bushy-bearded Quaker with a kewpie dollish tuft of hair on top, who operated a stop at his farm in Cass County. The Thomases then typically sent the fugitives on to Erastus Hussey in Battle Creek. Hussey started an anti-slavery newspaper, the Michigan Liberty Press. He owned a general store in Battle Creek and his house became one of the busiest stations on the Underground Railroad. In addition, Hussey was instrumental in organizing the Republican Party in the state and won a seat in the state senate in 1854, where he tried to pass a law making it illegal to capture runaway slaves in Michigan.

Elizabeth Margaret Chandler died just short of her 27th birthday from recurring fever, but wrote some of the most influential articles, essays and poems advancing the abolitionist cause of her day. She's said to have been the first woman writer to focus on abolishing slavery, but she also wrote

A portrait of Elizabeth Margaret Chandler.

articles promoting better treatment for American Indians.

As a child in Delaware, she lost both of her parents to illness by the time she reached age nine. Her grandmother raised her and her brother Thomas Chandler. She wrote and edited for abolitionist papers and magazines and participated in boycotts of goods produced by slave labor. In 1830, she and Thomas, along with an aunt, moved to Lenawee County near Adrian in the Michigan Territory just over the Ohio state line. A Quaker, she spearheaded the church's anti-slavery society there, and in 1832 established the Logan Female Anti-Slavery Society with her friend and neighbor Laura Smith Haviland.

She also helped popularize a widely reproduced image of a kneeling slave woman in chains with the phrase: "Am I not a woman and a sister?"

Chandler's most famous poem was titled "The Slave-Ship", a tearjerker about a man standing on the deck of a slave ship reflecting on the loss of his home, his status as a chief and warrior, and his beloved family. In the final verse, he decides to take back control of his fate:

"But ye shall — yes, again ye shall fondly embrace me!

We will meet my young bride in the land of the blest:

Death, death once again in my country shall place me,

One bound shall forever from fetters release me!"

He burst then, and sunk in the ocean's dark breast.

Chandler's short life ended on Nov. 2, 1834, of "remittent fever." She was buried near the family farm and her editor published two books of her writings after her death to raise money for the cause of abolition.

Several homes hid slaves in Ann Arbor, and the anti-slavery newspaper Signal of Liberty was published on Broadway Street and reached some 2,000 readers a week in the 1840s. Other Washtenaw County homes were stops as well, including some in Ypsilanti. Family names like Geddes and Starkweather lent out their homes to the effort.

The farm of Jehial and Mary Davis was one of several in and around Plymouth that participated in the Railroad, though the area was more a way station for the Port Huron destined than for those heading to Detroit.

George de Baptiste, a free-born Black man from Virginia, owned a barber shop and bakery in Detroit, and later bought a steamship, the T. Whitney. He smuggled runaways, including the Crosswhite family, to Canada on the Whitney.

Detroit's Second Baptist Church was the first Black-run congregation in the Midwest and came about in 1836, when 13 former-slave parishioners left the First Baptist Church due to discrimination. In 30 years, the church is said to have harbored 5,000 fugitives.

At first, it occupied a building on Fort Street, but moved in 1857 to its current location in Greektown. John Brown, Sojourner Truth and Frederick Douglass all visited, spoke to, or worked with the church. The church organized to gain the right to vote for African Americans, and established the state's first school for Black children.

Some former slaves hid at Finney's Hotel, at the southeast corner of Woodward and Gratiot avenues in downtown Detroit, owned by Seymour Finney, a thin man with a bright white moustache, who worked as a tailor and owned a tavern near Capitol Park (so named because it was the site of Michigan's first state capitol, before it moved to Lansing), and also near his own hotel and stable. While slave catchers drank in his bar and spilled their guts to him about their cruel but legal trade, cohorts sneaked in and out of Finney's nearby barn, which he used for coaches and coupes, at the northeast corner of State and Griswold streets. Sometimes the upstairs girls who worked at Finney's Hotel kept the bounty hunters entertained to distract them as the slaves they were after slipped across the river.

These are just some of the countless people who made the Underground Railroad work, and most remained devoted to it until the Civil War and the Emancipation Proclamation made it unnecessary.

MICHIGAN LYNCHINGS

In 2019, a park in Holt, south of Lansing, was renamed John Taylor Memorial Park in honor of a man who was lynched there in 1866. The park had been called Deadman's Hill, a callous reminder of the killing that occurred there.

John Taylor had been a slave in Kentucky, but was freed by Union troops during the Civil War. Now, just a year after the war ended, he was in Michigan, working as a farm hand.

He went to the farmhouse owned by his employer to ask for back wages, and in an argument is said to have hit three women with an axe. While none of the women died, rumors spread that Taylor had killed one of them. Taylor was arrested, but a mob stormed the jail where he was held and broke him out. They beat him and then murdered him.

Taylor's lynching was the first in Michigan of a horrible trend that swept through the country in the last part of the 1800s and well into the 1900s. Michigan's three known racial lynchings are dwarfed by the numbers in some other Midwestern states, notably Indiana, Iowa and Missouri, but together the killings are a reminder that Northerners were also guilty of racial mob violence.

The other two known incidents in Michigan involved allegations of rape against the lynching victims.

A medallion image similar to the one popularized by Chandler.

131

SLAVERS OF THE NORTH

AMERICANS TEND TO THINK OF SLAVERY AS A SOUTHERN THING, SINCE DIXIE HELD ONTO IT THE LONGEST AND LET IT GROW INTO A CENTRAL PART OF THEIR SOCIETY, CULTURE AND ECONOMY.

Yet northerners shouldn't be too smug. In Detroit, some of the best-known names of the pre-statehood era owned African or Native American slaves. Their names now sit atop street signs, on government buildings, and on maps as counties, towns and parks. Woodward Avenue, Macomb County and Wayne State University all have rich meaning here and beyond. Yet practically none of the connotations they conjure up to current Michiganders have to do with the guys who lent them their last names.

In the late 1700s, slavery in Michigan appeared to be a growing trend. Ste. Anne de Detroit Catholic Church records showed that in the 1760s, there were 82 slaves registered in the city, two-thirds of whom were identified as "Panis," a derogatory name for Native American women and girls. Twenty years later, the census listed 170 slaves as living in the city. Also, the intersection of two of the slaveholder-named roads, Woodward and Jefferson, was once the site of a public whipping post.

When the French ruled the area, most slaves in the state were Indigenous people, but after the Revolutionary War, British soldiers freed many Black slaves in areas further south and the former slaves fled to the north. For some it was out of the frying pan and into the fire. The Macomb family—the one after whom the county was named—and others took that as an opportunity to increase their own stock of slaves.

In 1787, the Northwest Ordinance formed Michigan and other future states into the Northwest Territory and outlawed slavery in the newly designated jurisdiction. Yet while Michigan was now officially part of the United States, the British still occupied the area. The U.S. was broke after the war, so they couldn't very well enforce the ban on slavery in the north, and the Brits pretty much let it slide.

Slaves, particularly Black slaves, became a status symbol among the wealthy of Detroit. Black slaves were less likely to run away than Indigenous people for the simple reason that they didn't have a nearby community to hide and protect them.

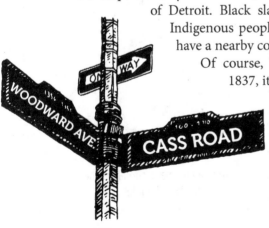

Of course, when Michigan achieved statehood in 1837, it was admitted as a free state and that put an end to people keeping slaves, at least out in the open.

The following are some of the people who lent their names to familiar places in the state, yet whose lives and considerable achievements are tainted by the fact that they owned people.

AUGUSTUS WOODWARD

Woodward Avenue is arguably the most famous road in Detroit. Its diagonal path bisects the city into its east side and west side. It passes through the bustling entertainment district, past the Fox Theatre, the gleaming 21st Century homes of all four major sports teams, past grand churches and some blighted neighborhoods, the broad, industrial historic Highland Park plant where Ford changed the world, past a porno palace, then the old State Fairgrounds, before crossing 8 Mile, and continuing on through several suburbs.

Now, quickly, tell me the full name of the guy after whom the road was named. Yeah, I didn't think you could.

Augustus Brevoort Woodward was a pointy-bearded, pointy-nosed lawyer who arrived in Detroit after President Thomas Jefferson named him the chief justice of the Michigan Territory. While he was on his way to Detroit, the fire of 1805 reduced the town to smoldering ashes. Nobody knows how the fire started, though it was likely an accident, and it wiped away just about every vestige of the city's colonial past under the French and British flags.

Augustus Woodward, chief justice of Michigan Territory and namesake of one of Detroit's main thoroughfares, made rulings favorable to runaway slaves, but also kept a Native American man as his own slave.

Woodward may have been disappointed when he saw the ruins over which his bench would rule, though he is credited with helping rebuild the city after the catastrophe. For one thing, he had the idea to plot the roads in a similar way to those in Paris and Washington, radiating out of a center point like spokes on a wheel, starting at the river. Fitting, then, that the main spoke would bear his name. He also helped found the University of Michigan, which began in Detroit and was later moved to Ann Arbor. In addition, he was the first appointee to the Michigan territorial Supreme Court and its chief justice.

Those achievements earned accolades for the highly educated Woodward, who spoke and wrote in several languages. People were impressed, if sometimes confused or put off, by his extensive and showy vocabulary, and the decisions Woodward wrote as a judge were said to be brilliant.

Yet people kept their distance from him for another reason: He stank. In contrast to his intellectual refinement, his personal hygiene was anything but

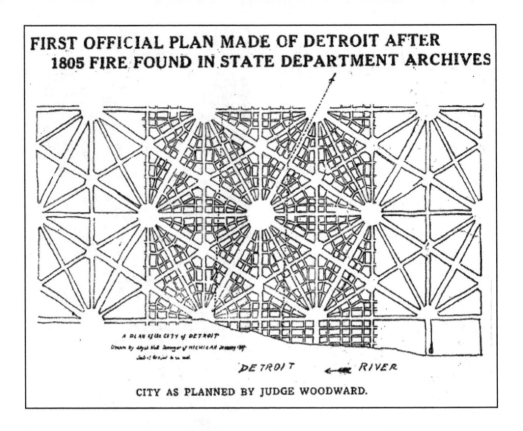

A PLAN if the CITY of DETROIT

Drawn by Abijah Hull Surveyor of MICHIGAN January 1807

Submit Gerald & co nink

DETROIT   RIVER

CITY AS PLANNED BY JUDGE WOODWARD.

refined. Even in a time before indoor plumbing and stores with shelves upon shelves of soaps, shampoos and deodorants, Augustus Woodward stood out for his pungency. He rarely bathed, people said, and when he did, it might be outdoors in a chair while it was raining. And don't even get them started about his breath.

What's more, Woodward was known to enjoy whiskey, having appeared on the bench with a detectable, alcoholic glow at times. The court in those days even did its business in a tavern on occasion. It was also not uncommon to find him lying drunk on the lawn of the courthouse after lunch on a warm day.

Yet in his views on race, Woodward was a White supremacist, sharing some of Jefferson's opinions that the non-White races were inherently inferior, and should be kept subservient. "They must be hewers of wood and drawers of water forever," Woodward wrote. "At any rate, they must not be put on a par with that dignified being a White man."

Still, he wrote opinions, based on existing law, that advanced the freedom of Black people in Detroit and the anti-slavery cause. When Canadian Richard Pattinson asked the territorial court to order two slaves returned to him after they fled to Detroit, Woodward ruled that they would remain free in Michigan. That ruling is said to have guaranteed that Michigan Territory would indeed follow the lead of the Northwest Ordinance in seeing that slavery would disappear here as a legal institution.

Ah, but he is on this list for a reason. In a classic case of do-as-I-say-not-as-I-do, Woodward himself owned a slave. He is said to have held an elderly Pawnee man as his servant, one of the last slaves in the city, until Woodward left Detroit in 1824.

LEWIS CASS

Lewis Cass is the namesake of Cass County and its county seat Cassopolis, as well as Cass Avenue and Cass Tech high school in Detroit. He was Michigan territorial governor and a U.S. Senator among other things. Belle Isle in the Detroit River is named after his daughter (the Belle part, that is).

Cass was also a slave owner and made it a priority to remove Native Americans from the Great Lakes region. Cass sold a slave by the name of Sally to the Macomb family, said to be the largest slave-owning family in Michigan history.

President James Madison—a slave owner himself—appointed Cass the second governor of the territory. In that capacity, Cass was determined to sing the praises of the land which he was charged to administer. Particularly, he was ticked off that government surveyor Edward Tiffin had deemed the state land not worthy to award to homesteading War of 1812 veterans. Tiffin based his assessment on a limited excursion to a swampy, mosquito-infested area on the western end of Lake Erie, near where

Lewis Cass was a territorial governor and also made his mark in Washington, D.C. Cass owned slaves and supported a law to mandate the return of runaway slaves. In 2020, Michigan's Gov. Whitmer removed Cass' name from a state government office building.

Monroe is now. Tiffin's bad-mouthing affected the rest of the country's opinion of the new territory, so Cass put together a group that included Henry Rowe Schoolcraft to explore the region and spread the word about Michigan's more habitable, farmable, huntable and fishable areas.

Cass had grand visions of the area he represented, whether because he actually believed it, or because his vanity would not let him hold the opinion that he was governor of a non-productive cesspool. Of course, Cass was also of the prevailing attitude of the time that the American Indians had to go, in order to make Michigan into the agricultural and industrial behemoth of his visions. Between 1817 and 1828, he strived to persuade Aboriginal tribes to give up most of the land in the states surrounding the Great Lakes.

After serving as territorial governor, Cass went on to represent Michigan in the U.S. Senate and serve on the cabinets of presidents Andrew Jackson—also a slave owner—and James Buchanan. He was the 1848 Democratic candidate for president, but lost to Whig candidate Zachary Taylor. Taylor owned slaves as well, yet he opposed attempts to expand the practice to new states or territories. Cass turned off the anti-slavery Democrats by pushing "popular sovereignty," the position that newly admitted states should decide for themselves whether to allow slavery.

He later also supported the Fugitive Slave Act of 1850, which required the return of slaves to their owners, even when they had made it to a free state.

135

The Macomb name is on a county, on this statue in Detroit, and several other places. At one time, the Macombs owned more slaves than anyone in Michigan.

JOSEPH CAMPAU

Joseph Campau Avenue runs northwest from the General Motors assembly plant in Hamtramck to Conant Street. Usually abbreviated as Jos. Campau, a section of the road in downtown Hamtramck is on the National Register of Historic Places for its mostly 1920s era commercial architecture.

Campau is said to have been the first millionaire in the state, having made his bucks in the early 1800s through real estate. He also owned a busy urban general store, making him one of the biggest local taxpayers of his time.

The Campau family came here from Montreal, where they had been among the leading slaveholders of that city in the 1600s. They arrived in Detroit in the early 1700s, and continued to own slaves through many generations. Many of their slaves were Native Americans.

THE MACOMB FAMILY

Macomb County, north of Detroit, became a national political bellwether when it became known as ground-zero for blue-collar Reagan Democrats, or long-time Democrats who strongly supported Republican Ronald Reagan.

It got its name from the Macomb family, a Scots-Irish clan who came to the New World in the mid-1700s. They first settled in Albany, N.Y., and then brothers William and Alexander moved to Detroit. The two brothers amassed a great amount of land, much of which was from "grants" from Indigenous people. They outfitted troops marching into Ohio, in case the war came that far west. For a while, the family owned Belle Isle, before they sold it to the Campau family.

Eventually William Macomb became Detroit's largest slaveholder. Not only did they own slaves, but in 1789, they got into the business of buying and selling them for people who were also in the market to own people.

William also bought Grosse Ile, the largest island in the Detroit River, from the Potawatomis. A slave named Charlotte took care of the Macomb family's mansion on the island, where they spent the summer. They also had one of the strip farms closest to Fort Detroit, where they spent the winter.

After William died, his widow Sarah Macomb bought "Molly the Wench" for $70, as she listed in her expenses.

Steel engraving of Anthony Wayne by Alonza Chappel.

"MAD ANTHONY" WAYNE

Michigan's most heavily populated county was named after a general who chased the British from Michigan and the rest of the Northwest Territory in the late 1700s, and later moved to Georgia to own slaves and run a plantation.

Anthony Wayne was a rowdy kid from Pennsylvania, who later distinguished himself in the army as a fierce and courageous fighter. In addition to fighting the British occupation of Michigan, he commanded the U.S. forces in the Northwest Indian War.

In Georgia, he broke a British alliance with Native American tribes there, and negotiated peace treaties with the tribes. For that, he was awarded a rice plantation, where he bought 47 slaves to do the labor.

He died in 1796, while returning to Pennsylvania from a military assignment in Detroit.

MILLION DOLLAR CON MAN GETS DESPERATE (KIDNAPPING TO KEEP A PROMISE OR JUST TRUST ME)

WHERE: TRAVERSE CITY, PETOSKEY, AND A TRAIL OF CRIME IN INDIANA, KENTUCKY AND NORTH CAROLINA
WHEN: MID-1980s–2000s

ARTHUR J. CURRY CAME TO PETOSKEY AND TRAVERSE CITY IN THE MID-1980s, AND SAW PROMISE IN A LANDMARK HOTEL IN EACH CITY. Both needed sprucing up to bring them back to former glory. Curry was a big player in a Chicago stock brokerage firm, and local leaders saw huge possibilities when speaking with the man in a business suit, who sported a close-cropped beard and glasses.

He proceeded to win the confidence of some of Petoskey's and Traverse City's movers, shakers and deep pockets. They'd written him huge checks and agreed to partner with him in buying and breathing life back into those towns' signature hotels, the Perry Hotel in Petoskey and TC's Park Place.

But the plans had begun sputtering. Curry was broke, and the two high-profile projects he'd put together were bankrupt. Investors started to get antsy, and several probably choked on their coffee as they saw the news of how he planned to get back in the black....

Gayle T. Cook, executive of a medical device manufacturer, returned to her Bloomington, Ind., home from grocery shopping on a Wednesday afternoon. She and her husband William Cook had started the company in their home in 1963, and 25 years later, had earned a spot on Forbes Magazine's list of the 400 wealthiest Americans.

That's why a desperate man stepped out of the shadows and pointed a gun at Gayle on that March afternoon in 1989.

The man, Arthur J. Curry, ordered her into a car that he had stolen at nearby Indiana University. He drove that car to a parking lot, pushed her inside of a van and gagged her, blindfolded her with duct tape and taped her to a chair.

It was all smiles and handshakes when Arthur J. Curry stepped in to save landmark hotels in Petoskey and Traverse City. When money got tight for Curry, though, he turned to kidnapping and bank robbery. (The Times Herald, March, 19, 1989)

For 36 hours, she experienced hell, breathing only through her nose while being driven around Bloomington.

He called William Cook to tell him that if he wanted his wife back, he needed to get the kidnapper $1.2 million in cash and a half mil in gold. The kidnapper sent him to a series of different phone booths with orders, finally asking him to leave the ransom cash and gold in a car parked at a Budget Rent-A-Car. FBI agents followed Cook around to the various pay phones and were able to trace one of the calls.

Then, agents traced a call to a pay phone close to where they were. When they reached the phone, they saw the apparent kidnapper just hanging up and getting into a van. When the van pulled away, they followed it. The van went into a Kmart parking lot and then proceeded behind the department store. Curry had seen the agents follow him, so he stopped the van and came out with his hands up.

When northern Michiganders heard of his arrest, they were stunned and a bit embarrassed to have been taken in by a crook who could be driven to such things. Was it the two bankruptcies? He'd left both projects, so that probably wasn't it.

But Curry didn't stop there.

His northern Michigan contacts would learn more about their friend who had blown into town, promised big things, bankrupted their joint project and then skipped town. And every time it would seem to be over, he was somewhere else, getting into more trouble.

A judge sentenced him to 30 years in prison for the kidnapping charge. He served 11 years of that, before he was paroled in 2001.

He stayed with a friend in Wabash, Ind., and started wheeling and dealing again in no time. He rubbed elbows with that town's influencers and bought some buildings and businesses. Apparently, the people of Wabash didn't question his past, and Curry started a construction firm with his brother Daniel Curry.

One night in a bar in a nearby town, he and brother Dan drank and argued. It heated up and Arthur stormed out and stole a car. When police caught up with him and pulled him over, he jumped out of the car and begged police to shoot him. After he made bail, he skipped town.

The next time he surfaced was in 2006, in Greensboro, N.C., where he'd been living in a boarding house. He told other

The Park Place Hotel is a Traverse City landmark. It had hit hard times in the 1980s, when Curry stepped in, offering to bring it back to life.

residents he was a millionaire with an Ivy League pedigree. He spoke of big business plans, and once again, talked people into investing in his projects.

He promised one of the residents he could help him receive government disability benefits, but instead of helping the man, he helped himself to his Social Security number and his identity.

Another town became stunned when U.S. attorneys caught up with him in North Carolina with indictments for him and his brother. They were wanted for robbing four banks in Indiana of more than $1 million over the previous three years. The Feds suspected them of another three bank jobs in Indiana and Kentucky, in which the methods and the witness descriptions matched the other heists: Men wearing hoodies and disguised with fake beards and moustaches. That would put the total take at about $2 million.

The robbers had been unusually successful, and had been able to speed away with such large sums of cash because they'd apparently had steely enough nerves to wait the extra time it took for tellers to give them cash from the vault, rather than running off after receiving the money from their teller-window drawers.

And yet, the mistake that brought police to their doorsteps was when Daniel spent some of the money at a casino. The bills aroused pit bosses' suspicion because they were splattered with red stains. The stains were from dye that had exploded on the money from commonly used devices that tellers put into stolen money to render it unusable and help identify robbers.

If that's not jaw-dropping enough, Daniel Curry also tried to deposit large amounts of cash, including a bunch of stained bills, into various banks in Indiana. Sometimes, he said he won the money in a poker game, and at other times, he said he washed it with red clothes—creating a new definition of money laundering.

Police searched Daniel's home in Indiana and found more stained money, disguises and other incriminating evidence. Officers in North Carolina also raided Arthur's residence and found red-dyed cash and other evidence.

Arthur pleaded guilty to the armed robberies and was sentenced to 22 years in prison.

Daniel decided to fight the charges and ended up in trial, a strategy that didn't work to his advantage. He received a sentence of 89 years.

PREDATOR'S FANTASY ISLAND

WHERE: NORTH FOX ISLAND
WHEN: 1970s

MANY PEOPLE DREAM OF OWNING AN ISLAND, OR A PIECE OF AN ISLAND, FOR THE ISOLATION AND PEACE OF LIVING APART FROM THE BUSTLE, NOISE AND CROWDS OF SOCIETY. On many of the 35,000 or so islands in the Great Lakes, countless people enjoy the good life, basking in nature and solitude.

However, in the 1960s and '70s, an Ann Arbor millionaire used the seclusion of North Fox Island to prey on children away from the prying eyes of the public.

Francis D. Shelden, a real-estate developer, bought the island in northern Lake Michigan in 1960 for $20,000, which is equivalent to about $175,000 today, and built an airstrip on it. Because he was a pilot and owned a twin-engine Piper airplane, he was able to fly it back and forth between the island and Charlevoix Municipal Airport in relative obscurity. He made a lot of friends in Charlevoix over the years and took several of them hunting on the island. Many of them were shocked in 1976, when the results of a state police investigation became public.

It seemed that on his plane trips, Shelden was taking boys—some as young as seven—to the island to molest them. But it was more complicated than that, bad as it was. Sheldon had set up a so-called charity under the name Brother Paul's Children's Mission, and convinced mostly needy parents to allow their children to go to the island for the "opportunities" it provided. The group also targeted runaways. Shelden and his cohorts said the children could learn about nature, camping, go on hikes, and learn to swim at the island mission. In reality, he and his accomplices made child pornography with the kids unfortunate enough to go there. "Sponsors" would donate to the organization, and in return they'd receive pornographic images and films produced there. Some also paid to fly to the island and molest the children themselves.

Francis D. Shelden owned North Fox Island in the 1970s and convinced people he was bringing children there for camping and educational opportunities. Later, it became clear that he had an elaborate child pornography and sex-abuse operation there. (Detroit Free Press, Dec. 12, 1976)

Shelden also had major investments in oil, ski resorts, and several real estate holdings. He set up shell companies to hide his activities and to avoid taxes. In addition, he sponsored similar organizations—including one in Tennessee—that were also set up to abuse children. He often took youths to accompany him on trips, and is said to have been a leader in producing child pornography in the Detroit area.

Others worked in the shadows with him, including Gerald Richards, a Catholic-school gym teacher and a magician Shelden met through a pedophilia magazine. Richards recruited boys to take to the island, and participated in the abuse. Dyer Grossman, a science teacher from New York was said to have been

part of it, and advised others on how to set up similar organizations to hide the trafficking of children.

In fact, the Shelden empire turned out to be just part of a nationwide network of pedophiles.

As police closed in on the group, and Richards in particular, he alerted the leader, and that's pretty much the last anybody here ever saw of Francis Shelden. Officers arrested Richards on July 23, 1976. He received a sentence of 2 to 10 years for raping a 10-year-old boy.

Before his arrest, though, Richards said he destroyed all the child porn in Shelden's office to save Shelden's family from shame and embarrassment. Shelden also had his Ann Arbor home emptied of anything damning, and

Shelden's snow-covered car sits at Charlevoix airport, abandoned after police caught up with his child-abuse ring and he fled to the Netherlands. (*Traverse City Record Eagle*, Dec. 18, 1976)

sent letters resigning from the board of directors for Cranbrook Institute in Bloomfield Hills and from the board of a residential center for emotionally disturbed boys in Farmington Hills.

He is believed to have flown to the Netherlands, where he was reported to have died in Amsterdam on Sept. 5, 1996.

Many have wondered if there was a connection between Shelden's island of horror and the still unsolved Oakland County child killings of the 1970s. The molestations and killings of four children—two boys and two girls ages 10 to 12—between February, 1976 and March, 1977, have never been solved. The four victims each disappeared from four to 19 days before being found killed and discarded. Could they have been

flown to the island, used and abused, before being dumped in the Metro Detroit area?

The timeline doesn't entirely support that theory, since only the first murder occurred before police arrested Richards and closed down the island, leaving Shelden to flee. Yet there were others who were believed to have been associated with Shelden who have been suspected. Most notably, Christopher Busch. The son of a General Motors executive, he was a convicted pedophile who copped a plea in another case. He was questioned in the Oakland County killings, and failed a polygraph test, but was released. He died in his parents' Bloomfield Township home in 1978, and his death was ruled a suicide.

CHARLEVOIX PRIVILEGE TO CHICAGO JOY KILLER

WHERE: CHARLEVOIX, CHICAGO
WHEN: 1924

IN NORTHERN MICHIGAN, MANY PEOPLE REMEMBER WITH FONDNESS GOING TO CONCERTS ON THE GROUNDS OF CASTLE FARMS. In the 1980s and '90s, it played host to acts like Aerosmith, Tina Turner and Ozzy Osbourne. Now, the palatial, multi-turreted, stone mansion on Lake Charlevoix—complete with a fountain, a pond and a large, outdoor model train—is available to rent for high-end weddings and other upscale events.

Yet there's a dark shadow over the estate's history. A young man who spent his summers there in the early 20th Century, went on to infamy for a monstrous murder.

Richard Albert Loeb was one half of a criminal pair now known as Leopold and Loeb. Loeb and his college chum Nathan Freudenthal Leopold Jr. killed 14-year-old Bobby Franks because they could. They did it for kicks, figuring they'd get away with it because of their supposedly superior intellects and their elevated stations in society.

Loeb's father, Albert Henry Loeb, was a lawyer and vice president of Chicago-based Sears, Roebuck & Co., the retail giant of its day. The company sold everything from watches to cars to entire homes in a kit. Yes, Sears eventually had retail stores, but its revolutionary beginning was its catalog. It was truly the Amazon of its day, allowing Americans in even the most remote places to order the latest in furniture, radios, musical instruments—you name it.

Charlevoix was becoming a favorite resort spot for the well-to-do, but there were already a good deal of farmers in the area. So, Albert Loeb set up a state-of-the-art dairy farming operation at Castle Farms to showcase what farmers could do with the latest equipment ordered from Sears & Roebuck.

His son Richard was a gifted student, allowing him to skip several grades in school. Richard graduated from the University of Michigan at age 17—the youngest student ever to attend the university at that point—and then went on to graduate studies in history at the University of Chicago.

While Richard Loeb spent the summers of his youth in Charlevoix, he spent the rest of the year in Chicago. He and Nathan Leopold both grew up in a section known as Kenwood. Leopold's parents were wealthy German Jewish immigrants, and he was also a child prodigy, said to be fluent in five languages. As a college student, he was already gaining a reputation for his work in ornithology, including being one of a handful of ornithologists to study the Kirtland's Warbler, a rare bird that summers in the central Lower Peninsula. He planned to go to Harvard after finishing at the University of Chicago.

While the two knew each other from a young age, they became friends at the university, where they discussed philosopher Friedrich Nietzsche's theories of the superman, believing that they themselves fit his definition. Richard and Nathan were also fascinated with crime, and believed that they had the mental capacity to commit the perfect crime.

They started by committing petty thefts and other crimes, which they got away with. That emboldened them to commit arson—for which they were never charged. That whetted their appetites for the big one. To prove their superiority, they needed to commit murder.

After months of planning, they targeted Bobby Franks, Loeb's second cousin and the son of a wealthy watch manufacturer. They rented a car under an assumed name and on May 21, 1924, themselves still teenagers, talked Franks into getting in the car for a ride home from school. The two criminals afterwards disagreed on who drove and who actually killed the teenager. But while they talked to their victim and drove around, one of them, from the back seat, reached up to the front and struck Bobby several times in the head with a chisel. Next, they pulled over and suffocated him until he died. They drove to Indiana and, after dark, dumped the boy's body in a culvert near the town of Hammond. They removed the boy's clothes, poured acid on his face to conceal his identity and

The victim, Bobby Franks.

A ransom note that Leopold and Loeb wrote on a stolen typewriter.
Their victim was already dead when they typed the note.

on his genitals so nobody could tell he was circumcised—another identifying detail.

When they got back to Chicago, they cleaned out the car, and typed a ransom note on a stolen typewriter. They made some calls under assumed names, but otherwise tried to carry on as usual. The body was soon found and identified and police made the case a top priority.

The problem was that Leopold couldn't help himself. He had to tell others his opinion of the horrific crime. He, with his supposed superior intellect, even said to a detective, "If I were to murder anybody, it would be just such a cocky little son of a bitch as Bobby Franks."

Then, a pair of glasses found near the body with unusual hinges on them turned out to be Leopold's. And eight days after the murder, police took the two young geniuses in for questioning.

First Loeb confessed, and then Leopold followed.

They stood trial, with the Loeb family hiring famous lawyer Clarence Darrow to head the defense team. Darrow was a staunch opponent of the death penalty, and made it his focus to avoid capital punishment for them, since their guilt was no longer in doubt.

The two were sentenced to life plus 99 years. Loeb's father died of a heart attack a month after the sentence was handed down.

On January 28, 1936, a fellow inmate stabbed and sliced Loeb in the shower more than 50 times with a straight razor. He died in the prison hospital.

Leopold served until March 1958, when he was paroled. He died of a heart attack on August 29, 1971, at age 66.

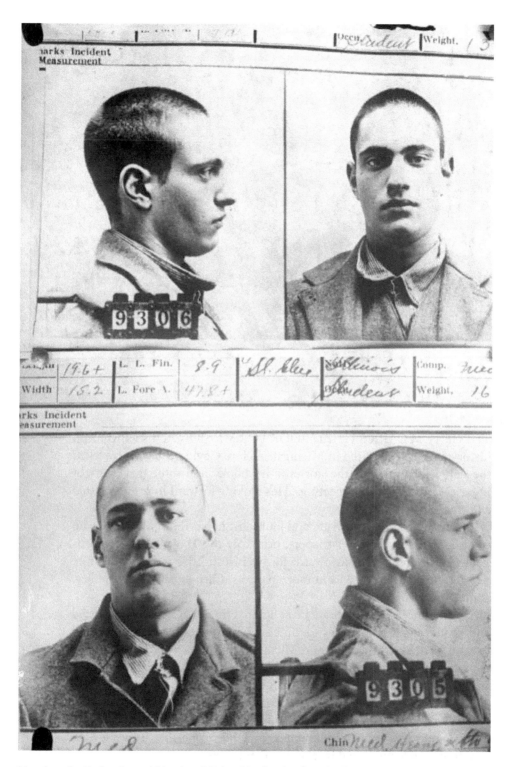

Mugshots for Nathan Leopold (top) and Richard Loeb, who thought their "superior intellect" would let them get away with murder.

THIS IS TOM CARR'S THIRD BOOK FOR MISSION POINT PRESS on history and/or true crime in Michigan. Before Covid-19 hit, he travelled the state telling many of the stories in his books, and some that aren't, at libraries and service club meetings. He's looking forward to resuming that after the pandemic subsides.

Carr is an independent writer and journalist in Northern Michigan who spent 25 years in daily newspapers, primarily the Traverse City Record-Eagle. He's won journalistic awards for his investigative reporting, feature writing, breaking news and humor columns. Carr often covered police, courts and crime.

As a freelancer, Carr has branched out into other media and has reported and produced several stories for Interlochen Public Radio and has had his work broadcast on NPR and Michigan Radio, as well. His work has appeared in the Detroit Free Press, the New York Daily News, traverseticker. com, Traverse Magazine and other media.

Tom Carr is author of *Blood on the Mitten: Infamous Michigan Murders, 1700s-Present, MI BAD: Robbers, Cutthroats & Thieves in Michigan's Past & Present* and was a contributing writer for *Inside Upnorth*, a Traverse City area travel guide published by Mission Point Press.

Carr lives and quarantines near Buckley, Michigan with his wife, Maria, where they raised their two sons.

ACKNOWLEDGMENTS

Writing a book means spending hundreds of hours alone in a room somewhere, staring at a laptop screen looking for just the right word, or pacing with a legal pad or computer tablet, while trying to ignore the Facebook and news notifications that ding on the screen. Even as I write about something that greatly interests me, it can put my attention span to the test.

Fortunately, however, I can't write a non-fiction book in a vacuum, so I do come in contact with others, without whom I would have no book. I would like to thank all of those people who helped out in some way, and I hope I don't forget anyone.

First, I thank my wife Maria, who prods me, checks my tone and encourages my writing, even when I'm a grumpy, sleepless wreck because of it.

I'd also like to thank Mission Point Press, including Anne Stanton and Heather Shaw, longtime friends who have given me encouragement from the start, and for Heather's talent in designing my books, giving them a cohesive and appealing look that is often the first thing to draw people to them. Thank you to Doug Weaver, who runs this great publishing company with Heather and Anne, and is the one who provides invaluable help after I write the books and start selling them. Special thanks to the editing talents of Susanne Dunlap and Hart Cauchy, who helped me smooth out many of the rough spots. And as always, thanks to Jodee Taylor for her help in marketing and her never-flagging sense of humor.

For help with research and providing information, I extend my appreciation to Gerald Micketti and Mark Thompson and the Presque Isle County Historical Museum; to Chriss Lyon and the Berrien County Sheriff's Department; to historian and author Larry Massie; and to office staff of the United States Department of Labor with help on certain statistics.

Some of the best stories in my books are ones about which people have steered me towards. A few have told me wonderful historical tidbits at author events, and they don't always leave their names. Some of the tales I've told in this book and some will go in others. Among the people to thank here are Bruce Moody, Tim Coe, Anne-Marie Oomen, and Bob Downes.

Many thanks to Ronald Smith, who steered me to the story of Harry Bennett, and gave me a ride in the unique Ford Model A that Bennett had helped design for him to tool around the grounds of the Ford Rouge Plant.

Also, thank you to Coreene Kreiser, a friend, terrific neighbor and wonderful photographer. And thanks again to Leigh Wietsma, who taught me about marketing the books and booking appearances when my first book was released.

Thank you to my local library, the Traverse Area District Library, and to the Library of Michigan, and libraries in general for the irreplaceable service they provide to their communities and to society at large. I'm also forever grateful to the libraries, service groups and other organizations that have invited me to tell stories, and to interact with readers.

Many thanks to the people who collect, interpret and educate about the state's history through the dozens of local historical societies around the state. For this book, I'm particularly indebted to the Detroit Historical Society, the Historical Society of Saginaw County, as well as to the Michigan Women's Hall of Fame.

And most importantly, thanks to you, the reader, for making it all worthwhile. Your interest sustains me in so many ways.

SOURCES FOR THIS BOOK INCLUDE:

BOOKS

A Duty to Honor, a Duty to Remember: A Tribute to Michigan Sheriffs and Deputy Sheriffs Who Have Made the Ultimate Sacrifice, by Timothy Coe

A Killing in Capone's Playground: The True Story of the Hunt for the Most Dangerous Man Alive, by Chriss Lyon

Almost An Island: Early Histories of the Shoreline Settlements in Presque Isle County, by Gerald Micketti and Mark Thompson

Autobiography of Malcolm X, by Alex Haley

Berry, Me, and Motown, by Raynoma Gordy Singleton

Counterfeit Justice: The True Story of 19th Century Organized Crime, by Eric T. Alli

Daylight in the Swamp, by Robert W. Wells

Dr. John Harvey Kellogg and the Religion of Biologic Living, by Brian C. Wilson

Early Organized Crime in Detroit: Vice, Corruption and the Rise of the Mafia, by James A. Buccellato

Ford, the Men and the Machine, by Robert Lacey

Fords: An American Epic, by Peter Collier

Hidden History of Detroit, by Amy Elliott Bragg

History of the Ottawa and Chippewa Indians of Michigan, by Andrew J. Blackbird

In Hoffa's Shadow: A Stepfather, a Disappearance in Detroit, and My Search for the Truth, by Jack L. Goldsmith

Lynching beyond Dixie : American mob violence outside the South, edited by Michael J. Pfeifer

Michigan's Crossroads to Freedom: The Underground Railroad in Jackson County, by Linda Hass

Michigan's Lumbertowns: Lumbermen and Laborers in Saginaw, Bay City and Muskegon, 1870-1905, by Jeremy W. Kilar

Molitor: The Murder of a Northern Michigan King, by Mark Thompson

Outlaws of the Lakes: Bootlegging & Smuggling from Colonial Times to Prohibition, by Edward Butts

Pioneering Michigan, by Eric Freedman

Potawatomi Tears & Petticoat Pioneers, by Larry B. Massie

Red Man's Rebuke, by Simon Pokagon

Terror in the City of Champions, by Tom Stanton

The Dawn of Detroit: A Chronicle of Slavery and Freedom in the City of the Straits, by Tiya Miles

The Falcon, by John Tanner

The French Canadians of Michigan: Their Contribution to the Development of the Saginaw Valley and the Keweenaw Peninsula, 1840-1914, by Jean Lamarre

The Great Influenza, by John M. Barry

The Kelloggs: The Battling Brothers of Battle Creek, by Howard Markel

Three Bullets Sealed His Lips, by Bruce A. Rubenstein and Lawrence E. Ziewacz

War Under Heaven: Pontiac, The Indian Nations and the British Empire, by Gregory Evans Dowd

Wicked Bay City, Michigan, by Tim Younkman

ARTICLES AND WEB SITES

"20 Cars Wrecked in Muskegon Riot," Detroit Free Press, Aug. 6, 1919

"A Startling Story: Terrible Iniquities That a Judge Says are Practiced in the Northwest," The Post-Star, Glen Falls, N.Y., Monday, January 31, 1887

"All City Hunts Kidnapers," Chicago Sunday Tribune, May 25, 1924

"Argument of William H. Seward, in defence of Abel F. Fitch and others, under an indictment for arson, delivered at Detroit, on the 12th, 13th and 15th days of September, 1851," University of Michigan Library

"Atrocious Crimes," The Northern Tribune, Cheboygan, Saturday, June 16, 1883

"Brothers indicted in bank heists," by Vic Ryckaert, Indianapolis Star, Thursday, May 11, 2006

"Constabulary Sent To Traverse City: Enforcement of Quarantine There Said to Require Armed Force," The State Journal, Lansing, Monday, January 20, 1919

"Death notices: Leebove," The Pittsburgh Press, Monday, May 16, 1938

"Detroit Dyer is Murdered: Polakoff Believed to be 'Taken for Ride in Labor Feud,'" The Windsor (Ontario) Star, Friday, March 23, 1928

"Earl Little's Death: E. Michigan Ave and Detroit St.," Malcolm X in Lansing, by Sarata Seydi projects.leadr.msu.edu/malcolmxinlansing/items/show/17.

"Encyclopedia of Detroit," detroithistorical.org

"Father of drug boss held on charge of beating," Detroit Free Press, Thursday, March 12, 1992

"Girls Hunted With Dogs: The Daughter of an Elmira Ex-Chief of Police Arrested in a Terrible Den in the West," The Buffalo (N.Y.) Sunday Morning News, January 30, 1887

"Henry Ford Repudiates Campaign Against Jews; Apologizes for Errors," The Wisconsin Jewish Chronicle, Friday, July 15, 1927

"Inflation calculator," officialdata.org

"Journey of the African: From the Atlantic Ocean to the Detroit River (series)," Detroit Free Press, February, 1996

"Key figure 'doesn't exist,'" Traverse City Record-Eagle, Monday, April 4, 1977

"Kidnaped Boy Died Fighting," Chicago Daily Tribune, Saturday, May 24, 1924

"Kidnap Rich Boy; Kill Him," Chicago Daily Tribune, Friday, May 23, 1924

"Leebove Killer Demands Hearing: Lawyer Hints Insanity May Be Defense," Port Huron Times Herald, Monday, May 16, 1938

"Lid Off On Campus," Detroit Free Press, Sunday, November 10, 1918

"Michigan News Tersely Told," (Bay City dateline), The Charlevoix County Herald, Friday, March 25, 1921

"Murder of Sen. Hooper, Graft Case Figure, Launches Record Manhunt in State; Was Witness Against McKay," The State Journal, Lansing, Friday, January 12, 1945

"Muskegon Probes Street Car Riots," Detroit Free Press, Friday, August 8, 1919

"On the Side, Edited by Earle R. Pitt," The State Journal, Lansing, Thursday, February 20, 1919

"Perry Hotel partner jailed: Kidnap charges filed in Indiana," by Perry Clark, Petoskey News-Review, Monday, March 20, 1989

"Porno charges jolt town: Millionaire frequented Charlevoix," by Jim Herman, Saturday, December 18, 1976

"Porno ring uses churches, tax laws," by Marilyn Wright, Traverse City Record-Eagle, Monday, April 4, 1977

"Rich Michigan Man Shot By Bandits: Franklin E. Parker, Bay City Lumberman, is Near Death," Detroit Free Press, Monday, September 4, 1916

"Several Loggers Killed by Dynamite," The News-Palladium, Benton Harbor, Thursday, April 21, 1887

"The 1866 lynching of John Taylor shows Michigan's role in America's history of racist violence," by Stateside staff, August 24, 2018, michiganradio.org

"The Great Railroad Conspiracy," by Bill Loomis, hsmichigan.org

"The Michigan Iniquity: Some Statements Going to Contradict the Woman, Minnie's Story," Pittsburgh Daily Post, Jan. 25, 1887

"The Rise and Fall of Harry Bennett," by Amy Wilson, June 3, 2003, Automotive News

"Transactions of the American Clinical and Climatological Association, 2008," by Walter J. Daly, M.D.

"White Slavery in the Northwoods: Early U.S. Anti-Sex Trafficking and its Continuing Relevance to Trafficking Reform," by Bonnie Schucha, William & Mary Journal of Race, Gender and Social Justice, Vol. 23, 2016-2017

"Year Passes; Still No Francis Shelden," The Herald-Palladium, Benton Harbor-St. Joseph, Friday, December 16, 1977

INDEX

DON'T MISS THESE OTHER BOOKS BY TOM CARR

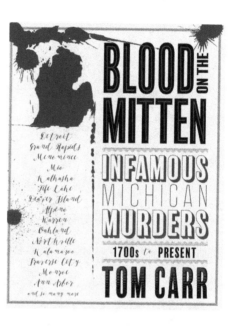

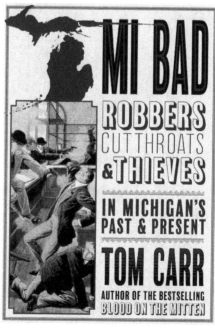

9 781950 659760